P9-BIY-157

Are We There Yet?, 2002

Dickie Landry

Composer. Saxophonist. Photographer. Artist.

August 22 – December 19, 2015

Curated by Susan Moldenhauer

Essays by Dickie Landry, Babs Case and Nicole M. Crawford

Funded in part by an anonymous donor, Edelweiss Funds, Rocky Mountain Power Foundation, University of Wyoming Art Museum Gala Funds, Wyoming Public Media, Wyoming Arts Council through the National Endowment for the Arts and the Wyoming State Legislature

Dickie Landry: Composer. Saxophonist. Photographer. Artist. is published on the occasion of the exhibition by the same title presented at the University of Wyoming Art Museum, August 22 - December 19, 2015. A companion exhibition, *Dickie Landry: Explorations in Axonometric Projection*, was presented at the Jackson Hole Center for the Arts, October 7 - November 9, 2015.

Dickie Landry: Composer. Saxophonist. Photographer. Artist. was presented at the University of Wyoming Art Museum. The exhibition, residency, and this publication were made possible by: an anonymous donor, Edelweiss Funds, Rocky Mountain Power Foundation, University of Wyoming Art Museum Gala Funds, Wyoming Public Media, Wyoming Arts Council through the National Endowment for the Arts and the Wyoming State Legislature

Dickie Landry: Explorations in Axonometric Projections was presented by the Art Association of Jackson Hole, Dancers' Workshop, Jackson Hole Center for the Arts, and the University of Wyoming Art Museum. The exhibition, residency, and this publication were made possible by: Pam Case & Larry Berlin, Center of Wonder, Dancers' Workshop Board of Directors, E/Ye Design, Pamela & Scott Gibson, Habits Jackson Hole, Hotel Terra Jackson Hole, Judy & Don Opatrny, Linda & Larry Perlman, Ann & Steve Ryan, Polly & Richard Spencer, Tayloe Piggott Gallery, US Bancorp, Barbara & John Vogelstein Foundation, Willow Street Group in memory of Stephen Adamson, Wyoming Arts Council, and Wyoming Humanities Council.

Cover: *Diamonds in Hand*, 2008

ISBN: 978-0-9630869-9-0

Dickie Landry in Wyoming

It might be surprising to know that the University of Wyoming Art Museum mounted the first major survey of Richard "Dickie" Landry's artwork. Known primarily for his work in music—as a composer, saxophonist, and producer—and with little connection to Wyoming, the opportunity to explore Landry's visual work came through a chance meeting in 2012.

Sculptor James Surls invited me to his Open Studio Weekend, which included a performance by Landry, well known as a saxophonist who has traveled the world creating solo musical responses to architectural spaces such as museums and cathedrals. His hour-long performance was mesmerizing, minimal, resonating in the gallery filled with Surls' newest wood and metal sculptures. Landry's ethereal and haunting music permeated the space as he ventured from one sculpture to the next, responding to each in an ongoing, continuous sound.

Introducing myself, I asked Landry if he had ever been to Wyoming and would he consider coming to the University Art Museum. "Sure" he replied. As we talked, it became clear to me that here was a remarkable person with an extraordinary story to tell. His photographic work from the New York scene in the 1970s was being developed as an exhibition in Lafayette, Louisiana, but his artistic oeuvre stretched across experimental work, drawing, and painting.

My first visit to Lafayette to see Dickie convinced me that telling his story would embrace his creative work in the visual arts, its place in art history, and enable interdisciplinary dialogue in the academic and public communities that the University of Wyoming Art Museum serves.

Susan Moldenhauer
Director & Chief Curator
University of Wyoming Art Museum

Dickie Landry plays to the Tetons. Photo by Babs Case.

Dickie Landry performing with *Sound Machine*, University of Wyoming, courtesy University of Wyoming Art Museum

In my own words

I first started thinking about New York City while I was in high school. I visited the library frequently to read books on composers and artists. Noticing that the books were published in Paris, London, or New York, I thought to myself, I can possibly walk to New York. But to get to Paris or London was out of reach.

In 1956, upon graduating from high school in the small village of Cecilia, Louisiana, a friend offered me a ride to NYC in his brand new red and white Corvette. The idea was to visit my brother and his friend, who were both enrolled at Columbia University. It was an epic ride. Before there was an interstate system in the U.S.... But that is a whole other story. Arriving in the city, we drove straight to the famous jazz club, Birdland. There we saw Miles Davis, Bud Powell, "Philly Joe" Jones, and many others. I was hooked.

I made several trips after that, usually by Greyhound bus. The summer of 1963 I decided to take flute lessons and wrote to a flute teacher by the name of Arthur Lora. He invited me up to study. The first question he asked was: "Why do you want to learn how to play the flute? To go to Juilliard, play in a symphony orchestra, or be a soloist?" My answer was: "I just want to learn how to play it." He accepted me as a student and recommended this: "We will start with one note at a time." Now remember, this is 1963, I'm a poor boy from Louisiana, and I am there for six weeks, for six notes. No way!! So, I practiced fourteen to sixteen hours a day. Three lessons later he said, "You don't know who I am, do you?" "No" I replied. "Do you know who Arturo Toscanini is?" he asked. I said, "Yes." Lora then informed me that he was Toscanini's principal flute player for fifteen years. My jaw dropped. Studying with Lora gave me the musical ability to perform Philip Glass's music, years later.

By late summer of 1963, I was back in Louisiana. On November 3 of that year I got busted in the biggest raid to date in the state, for growing marijuana on my family farm. If convicted, I would have to serve a mandatory twenty-five-year sentence at Angola State Penitentiary. To make a long story short, luckily, I somehow ended up with just probation. But I would not be unable to leave the state for five years. In hindsight, that was the best thing that could've happened to me. If I had moved to the city in January of 1964, as I had been planning, I would not have met any of the artists and composers who are in this exhibit.

In the end, my probation officer gave me six months off of the sentence. I immediately moved to NYC. It was January of 1969. At that time, I only knew two people, both of whom were from Louisiana... artist Keith Sonnier and composer/arranger William "Bill" Fischer. Little did I know that upon arriving in the city and beginning to work with them, I would be going to the top of the art and music world in one giant step. Keith Sonnier was with the Leo Castelli Gallery and Bill Fischer was the chief arranger at Atlantic Records.

Through Keith Sonnier I met Philip Glass and joined his newly formed Ensemble. Those first few months in the city, I met a lot of artists and composers. Through Bill Fischer, I met many of the great jazz and rhythm and blues musicians of the period who were recording for Atlantic Records. Bill got me a job there as a copyist, but I only lasted nine months in the corporate world. I decided that the budding downtown art scene was where I wanted to be working as a musician, videographer, composer, and photographer.

So begins my decade in the city. The avant-garde art scene was just about to explode after a period of abstract expressionism and pop art. I soon fell in with a crowd of artists, musicians, dancers, writers, and theater people that included, in addition to Sonnier and Glass, Robert Rauschenberg, Gordon Matta-Clark, Robert Smithson, Michael Heizer, Walter de Maria, Steve Reich, Jon Gibson, Laurie Anderson, Ulrich Rückriem, Susan Rothenberg, Mary Heilmann, Nancy Graves, Spalding Gray, Joan Jonas, Richard Serra, William S. Burroughs, Mabou Mines, Chuck Close, Robert Wilson, Lawrence Weiner, William Wegman, Joseph Kosuth, Bruce Nauman, Lucinda Childs, Trisha Brown, and Deborah Hay. These and so many others from that time are now considered visionaries in their respective fields.

There was no SoHo then. That area of town was nothing but block after block of boarded up small manufacturing businesses. A few artists were living in these spacious lofts, which was against the law at the time. They boarded up their windows so that the cops could not see the lights at night and arrest them. There was only one restaurant, Fanelli's, until Gordon Matta-Clark opened the artist-run restaurant, Food. There was Jeffrey Lew and his gallery at 112 Greene Street, which was one of the first alternative gallery spaces in the city. Many of the artists in this exhibit had their first shows at 112. It was open 24 hours a day and artists were free to do whatever they wanted to do with the space. By the mid 1970s art galleries started to move down into SoHo and the city legalized loft living.

It was the heyday of minimalism, pop art, sculpture, video, photography and conceptual art. Working and living in this atmosphere is what shaped my direction.

Richard "Dickie" Landry
Cecelia, Louisiana

“got your shoes on? are you ready?”

Dickie Landry paints, composes, plays music, photographs, and the fact that he is a fine cook should be added to his list of expression.

All art is an expression of some one person’s perception of existence. Whether that expression comes in the form of a painting, a piece of music, a dance, an architectural construction, a poem, engraving on a belt conch, a saddle, or the shaping of the bone handle of a knife, each creation reflects an understanding, a hope, a dream, a statement of the creator’s place and time in the world. Picasso said that art is the lie that makes us realize the truth.

No matter the geographic or temporal origin of a work of art, there is always some connection to all other artistic expressions. The prehistoric cave paintings in the south of France are not to be seen as unrelated to the music of Stravinsky or the poems of Emily Dickinson, or the jazz music of Charlie Parker. So, too, the great body of work by Dickie Landry, a prolific modern artist, photographer, composer, and musician from

Dickie Landry and Babs Case, Teton National Park, 2015

Louisiana, is a treat for the eye, the mind, and the imagination.

Dickie Landry’s photographic work documents a timeline of his relationships with others and with the world around him, specifically during his years in New York, beginning in late 1969 and continuing through the 1970s, at a time when even the New York downtown art scene was a wild “frontier.”

The stories of his own life are all there, hanging on the walls, speaking to us through sound and moving images, through the faces of those he loved and photographed, and his endless playful exploration of a single shape.

He is a keen observer and delights in the images of the lens, and through his lifetime of exploration he has always generously encouraged others to explore as well, in pursuit of their own perceptions and questions of the moment.

Dickie and I were friends from the moment we met...I guess you could say it was love at first sight. We spoke the same language of life and art. We have worked together on many projects and have supported each other as artists through many more. There is no one else on earth that I would rather walk the streets of New York City with. My heart is filled with many memories and I am very grateful to call myself a friend. He has influenced my life since the moment I met him.

“got your shoes on? are you ready?”

Babs Case
Artistic Director, Dancers’ Workshop
Jackson Hole, Wyoming

Experimentation, Collaboration and Community: 1970s New York Art Scene

The New York art scene of the 1970s was momentous in influencing change in the art world. However, it was only recently that this period has seen much academic attention. Artists and the commercial art market were at polar opposites. The 1970s saw the first sale of a contemporary artwork for more than $100,000 (1973, Scull Collection at Sotheby Parke Bernet[1]) while artists began to seek alternative modes of presenting outside the museum or commercial gallery. This short period marked a shift away from the elitism of the arts, and started a period in which performance was presented off the stage and art strayed from the gallery. These trends led to the development of multi-medium, interdisciplinary, experimental artists like Dickie Landry.

For New York, the 1970s mark a low point in its history. More than 820,000 people fled the crime-ridden city for the suburbs. New York City was on the verge of bankruptcy as Wall Street struggled under the economic stagnation of the era which left tens of thousands without work. Vacant buildings fell into disrepair and became home to squatters. The subway was unreliable and dangerous; muggings and rapes were reported on the trains and in the dark tunnels. The population dropped to less than 7.1 million, erasing four decades of growth, and by 1980 was only slightly higher than it was in 1930. Hit with an unprecedented financial crisis in 1975, the New York Police Department was forced to lay off 50,000 employees. The cuts continued for the next five years. The resulting shortage of law enforcement personnel combined with the energy blackout of 1977 set the stage for looting and arson throughout the city. New Yorkers were also terrorized by the serial killer David Berkowitz, known as "Son of Sam," and saw the face of the first missing child on a milk carton, Etan Patz, who disappeared in SoHo during a short walk to school.[2]

Even as the city was in crisis, there were indications that New Yorkers were banding together to create a new democratic vision for their city. The cultural side of New York, much smaller and more interconnected than today, was a breeding ground of new ideas and endless possibilities. Painters knew musicians who knew writers who connected and collaborated, stirring up a new range of

Dickie Landry, *Four Way Tenor Split*, 1974, 112 Greene St basement

Richard Serra, *Splashing*, 1969, Leo Castelli Warehouse, New York City

Food, exterior, 1972

possible ways in which the idea of art, and the experience of art, could be reconfigured. Commercial galleries were focused on self-perpetuation, and artists reacted against the commercial model by forming artist-run alternative spaces.

Unlike today, where we've become accustomed to renovated warehouse or factory exhibition spaces, artists inhabited these spaces out of necessity. SoHo was a major neighborhood for this repurposing. Starting in the late 1960s the neighborhood, located south of Houston Street and north of Canal Street, became a decaying hinterland of New York as companies moved to the suburbs for cheaper rents and larger spaces. The large buildings abandoned by industry became the perfect stage for performances and exhibitions. In an effort to persuade New Yorkers to populate this area, the city

Gordon Matta-Clark, *Four Way Walls*, 112 Greene St Galley, New York City

council offered artists a tax break, which allowed them to occupy these large spaces for creative use. [3] At this time commercial galleries and museums were generally located in Upper Manhattan in Midtown and the Upper East Side, a safe distance from the bedlam and turmoil of SoHo. For the artists, these abandoned industrial spaces provided enough room to live and work, creating the reality of loft living.

The process of producing art became integrated into the local community placing value on the ideas and process over the finished product. Artists activated redun-

Gordon Matta-Clark, *Time Well*, 1973, casting in basement of 112 Greene St

dant pieces of infrastructure and invented new landscapes through previously unused building facades, rooftops, foundations, and water towers. Artist Gordon Matta-Clark (1943-1978) was a key contributor to building this new community art scene. In the fall of 1971 he established the restaurant Food, on Prince Street, with his girlfriend, the artist and dancer Caroline Goodden, and artist Tina Girouard, partly to provide a much-needed space to eat and socialize. The communal artist-run restaurant became a place to gather and share ideas that hosted several food-based performances.

It was here that Matta-Clark created his first infamous building cuts; he described the process as "like a dance with a building."[4] Matta-Clark's large-scale building cuts, which consisted of dissected concrete walls and floors, became part of the pioneering practice that redefined how artists engaged with their surroundings. His work contradicted the distinction between sculpture and architecture. Using video, drawings, photographs, and film, Matta-Clark forged a new way of re-thinking medium-specificity. These contributions added a level of complexity that pressed the traditional limits of media.

The social aspect of the 1970s is undeniable, from places like Food to the emergence of alternative exhibition spaces that allowed for artistic experimentation of presentation and exhibition beyond the commercial gallery models. Spaces where artworks like Matta-Clark's building cuts had an opportunity to be born.

Experimental artist-run spaces date back to the Sculpture Center of 1928, formed in artist Dorothea Denslow's studio. However, the 1970s New York added a new dimension of frustration with the traditional commercial gallery model. 112 Workshop (or 112 Greene Street), the Kitchen, Artists Space, and Creative Time developed from this frustration. Several spaces addressed the neglect by the art establishment of cultural groups, and specific cooperative galleries were formed by women artists or were aligned with the Black Power movement. While each of the artists behind the new gal-

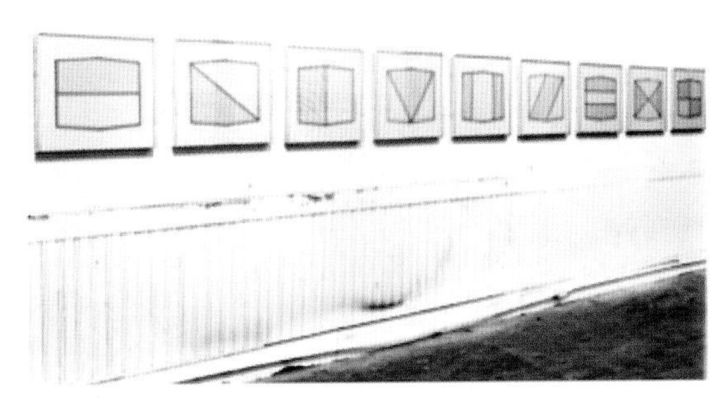

Dickie Landry, *Video Drawings*, 1970, 112 Greet St Gallery, New York City

leries sought to integrate discussion, flow of ideas, experimentation, exhibition, and process into the community, these spaces defied clear definition.

One of the best examples is 112 Workshop (or 112 Greene Street) that became the center of the community and encouraged cross-pollination between visual and performing arts. Founded in 1970 by Jeffrey Lew, Alan Saret and Matta-Clark, it resisted the label of "gallery," and was the first sizable independent art space in New York at the time. 112 Workshop was a place for artists to both create and exhibit works. It was primarily self-curated and did not have a formalized structure for exhibition schedules, sales, and fundraising. Lew ran the space democratically with his friends, "as an artist, for artists," [5] and never refused anyone artistic freedom even if it meant digging a hole in the basement or cutting into the walls. Matta-Clark, for example, used the site as a "creative laboratory."[6] While there is little published on the venue, much of the work from 112 Workshop no longer exists or was ephemeral to begin with. Although the space existed just a little over a decade, there is little doubt of the prodigious impact it had not only on its artists but on other alternative exhibition spaces, and on the art scene as a whole.

The last group exhibition at 112 Workshop to include a large number of the principal artists from the first years was *The Anarchitecture Show* in March 1974. The group, which met regularly at 112 Workshop, included Matta-Clark, Girouard, Goodden, Laurie Anderson, Suzanne Harris, Jene Highstein, Bernard Kirschenbaum and Richard Nonas, as well as Dickie Landry. The name was a

One Quart Exterior Latex Green Industrial Enamel Thrown on the Brick Wall (Weiner installation with Tina Girouard), 1973, digital print, 13 x 19 inches

I Love New York (Mary Heilmann), 1972, digital print, 13 x 19 inches

Glass in the Sky (Philip Glass), 1977, digital print, 19 x 13 inches

mixture of 'anarchy' and 'architecture' and conceived in informal conversation, one of the main ways the group collaborated. Contributions to the 1974 exhibition were anonymous to emphasize their collective approach to process. The group tackled ideas of architecture and its complicity in capitalist modes of production and used wordplay and found photographs to explore issues related to cities, inhabitation of buildings, and the role of property. [7] Richard Nonas said, "*The Anarchitecture Show* in 1975 was the last show a lot of us did together. I think we were all feeling the pull of the separate interests on the one hand and we were also sensing what was happening to 112 Greene Street as a space." [8] While the exhibition represented the culmination of the early experimental collaborative years that 112 Workshop was built upon, it also characterized how the artists grew from these relationships to work both collaboratively and independently.

The Chatham Square building with an open, communal, and creative atmosphere that greatly influenced the philosophy behind Food and 112 Workshop, emancipated visual and performance boundaries. Mary Heilmann, who lived in the building, described the space as a place where, "there was music going on...and all kinds of Jazz was played because of Dickie, and people on the street would call out to come up and participate in the music." [9] The space be-

Einstein on the Beach, Knee 2 (Robert WIlson / Philip Glass), 1976, digital print, 13 x 19 inches

Einstein on the Beach, Train 1, 1976, digital print, 13 x 19 inches

came a meeting place for the 112 Workshop community including musician Philip Glass. Recognized as one of the most prominent composers associated with musical minimalism, he founded the Philip Glass Ensemble with Landry in 1969.

In 1976, Glass collaborated with Robert Wilson, an avant-garde stage director and

Guggenheim Touch Up (Richard Serra), 1970, digital print, 13 x 19 inches

Object Situation Object (Keith Sonnier), 1969, digital print, 13 x 19 inches

playwright, to create an experimental performance that distorted the boundaries between music, dance, choreography, and visual art. *Einstein on the Beach* broke from the rules of conventional opera. Instead of a traditional orchestral arrangement, Glass chose to compose the piece using synthesizers, woodwinds, and voices of the Philip Glass Ensemble. The story unfolds using a series of powerful recurrent images shown in juxtaposition with abstract dance sequences created by choreographer Lucinda Childs, (b. 1940) who was interested in blurring the lines between dancers and non-dancers. The performance took place over five hours and there were no traditional intermissions. Instead, the audience was invited to wander in and out during the performance. [10]

It is important to acknowledge those artists from the late 1960s who began to bend the boundaries of media and set the stage for the 1970s. Artists such as Eva Hesse, Bruce Nauman, Keith Sonnier, Richard Serra, and Joel Shapiro radically transformed the way artists approached sculpture. The group of young artists used the detritus of modern society to create artworks that focused more on materials and process than the finished object. They challenged the traditional definition of sculpture by using various metals, machinery, plastic, bamboo, wood, and found objects to create works that explored connections to the environment, anthropology, and architecture. Sonnier was among the earliest artist to use neon light as a central element in his work. Sonnier described the period as, "...much more communal. It was the late '60s, there was a very different attitude toward artists and work. There was very little money involved. I mean, this is before contemporary art was sold for very large sums. I think we were amazed that what we were making would even be bought." [11]

Jones Beach Piece 1 (Joan Jonas & George Trakas), 1970, digital print, 13 x 19 inches

The communal approach to experimentation and collaboration allowed women artists to express their voice on par with their male counterparts. Joan Jonas - a pioneer of video and performance art who experimented with video, performance, installation, sound, text, and drawing - explored ways of seeing, the rhythms of ritual, and the authority of objects and gestures. She used video and

Self-Portrait, 1969, digital print, 19 x 13 inches

performance to break new ground as an innovative medium to a self-reflexive study of female identity. She purposely took the process away from the gallery walls by performing on site on locations such as Jones Beach in Long Island (collaborating with George Trakas, John Erdman, Carolyn Gooden and Susan Rothenberg) based on the idea that the perception of image and movement is altered by distance.

The history and legacy of the art scene of New York in the 1970s lives in the stories of those who were there. Jeffrey Lew stated, "To me, it was all about the experience. Galleries make money, and provide interior decorators with crap for rich people's houses. But I saw art as part of the community. Art is a community. Yet we weren't even thinking about that – we were in the middle of it. We were too busy to be thinking about concepts, [we] were creating them. And I believe that that's how concepts are derived – by physical activity, not intellectual thoughts." [12]

While there is little documentation and academic research on the period, Landry communicates the entire narrative through his own artwork, music, and photographs. Spending much of his time behind the camera, contributing regularly to performances and installations through music, and working closely with a wide variety of artists Landry provides a unique insider's perspective of the decade that influenced significant change in the art world.

Nicole M. Crawford
Curator of Collections

ENDNOTES

[1] Rita Reif, "Sculls' Art to be Sold at Auction," *The New York Times*, September 9, 1986 (The sale totaled $2,242,900, an auction record for post-World War II and Jasper Johns' 1965 *Double White Map* sold for $240,000.)

[2] Christine Sterbenz, "New York Used to be a Terrifying Place," *Business Insider*, July 12, 2013.

[3] Jessamyn Fiore, *112 Greene Street: The Early Years* (New York: Radius Books, 2015), 7.

[4] Esme Fieldhouse, "Laurie Anderson, Trisha Brown, Gordon Matta-Clark: Pioneers of the Downtown Scene, New York 1970s," *Blueprint*, May, 2011.

[5] Fiore, *112 Greene Street: The Early Years,* 7.

[6] Fiore, *112 Greene Street: The Early Years,* 77.

[7] "The Anarchitecture Group," The Spatial Agency, accessed April 25, 2016, http://spatialagency.net/database/the.anarchitecture.group.

[8] Fiore, *112 Greene Street: The Early Years,* 63.

[9] Fiore, *112 Greene Street: The Early Years,* 46.

[10] "Einstein on the Beach," Pomegranate Arts Projects, accessed April 25, 2016, http://www.pomegranatearts.com/project-einstein/index.html

[11] Max Blagg, "Keith Sonnier," *Interview Magazine*, November 30, 2008.

[12] Fiore, *112 Greene Street: The Early Years,* 29.

Dickie Landry, photo by Emma Novella

Dickie Landry
Composer. Saxophonist. Photographer. Artist.

University of Wyoming Art Museum *Dickie Landry, Composer. Saxophonist. Photographer. Artist.* begins with Landry's early work, made in New York City during the 1970s. It was a time of a burgeoning avant-garde scene as artists, musicians, composers, dancers, and performance artists rebelled against the accepted traditions and sought new ways of creative expression. The antecedents of the late 20th century developments in Minimalism, Performance Art, Conceptual Art, and Video came out of what was happening in Lower Manhattan at this time.

Landry (b. 1938), who was born in the bayou town of Cecilia, Louisiana, began playing saxophone at the age of 10. He had a curiosity and a passion for music and art, often visiting the local library to read about artists and composers. New York became a dream destination for Landry as early as high school. His first visit in 1956 was with a friend who drove him to New York in a new red and white Corvette. Their first destination was Birdland, the mecca for jazz at the time. He heard Miles Davis, Bud Powell, "Philly Joe" Jones, and others and knew New York was his destiny. In 1969, he made the move to New York where he met a crowd of young artists, musicians, dancers, writers, and performers that included Laurie Anderson, Trish Brown, William S. Burroughs, Lucinda Childs, Chuck Close, Jon Gibson, Philip Glass, Nancy Graves, Spalding Grey, Deborah Hay, Michael Heizer, Mary Heilman, Joan Jonas, Mabou Mines, Gordon Matta-Clark, Robert Rauschenberg, Steve Reich, Susan Rothenberg, Ulrich Rückrum, Richard Serra, Robert Smithson, Keith Sonnier, and Walter de Maria.

The nexus of these artists and their experimentations was 112 Greene Street, a gallery space owned by Jeffrey Lew and open to sculptors, painters, dancers, filmers, and performance artists. It was a space for complete freedom of expressions without direction, supervision, or curatorial oversight. The doors were never locked, artists had 24-hour a day access, and it became a catalyst and sounding board for new ideas. The first artists to explore architectural ideas and create large-scale, site-specific installations were Gordon Matta-Clark, Alice Aycock, Ned Smyth and George Trakas. New directions in painting included Susan Rothenberg's re-introduction of the image into contemporary painting and Mary Heilmann's hard-edge and gestural abstractions. Bill Beckley explored integrating the audience into his sound installation/performances and Chris Burden and Carolee Schneemann created interactive performance works. Dennis Oppenheim created unique forms of sculpture that explored multimedia concepts. Joan Jonas, Keith Sonnier, and Dickie Landry explored video projection and performance that laid the foundation for today's large-scale video installations. The gallery at 112 Greene Street became the place to see, hear, perform, and show contemporary art.

Landry garnered attention early in his New York days with his first exhibition and performance at Leo Castelli Gallery. He was exploring randomness, harmony, and repetition in photography and videotape. In his music, he was experimenting with improvisation, minimalism, and process which resulted in his pioneering use of quadrophonic delay, using the original sound with time delayed repeats, which enabled his solo work to become a quintet.

Landry's creative pursuits gave him a unique relationship to the new art of the time, both as participant and documenter. He was a member of the Philip Glass Ensemble, studio assistant to Richard Serra, participant in Keith Sonnier's studio experiments, performed with Steve Reich, and performed in Robert Wilson and Philip Glass' opera *Einstein on the Beach*, among many others. All along, he was documenting the artistic experimentations he experienced, creating what would be the single largest photographic collection of the period from an insider's viewpoint.

The University of Wyoming Art Museum, working in partnership with the Dancers' Workshop, Center for the Arts, and Arts Association in Jackson Hole, Wyoming mounted two exhibitions on Landry's artistic work. *Dickie Landry: Composer. Saxophonist. Photographer. Artist.* is a survey of his artwork and documentation photographs between 1970 and 2015. Presented at the University of Wyoming Art Museum, it builds on the exhibition *Dickie Landry's New York, 1970 – 1979,* an exhibition of his photographs, which premiered at the Paula and Lulu Hilliard University Art Museum, University of Louisiana, in 2014 and traveled to Salomon Contemporary, New York City, in 2015. *Dickie Landry: Explorations in Axonometric Projection* considers his use of the distinctive six-sided form that is fundamental to his visual vocabulary in drawing, experimental photography, and painting. That exhibition was presented at the Jackson Hole Center for the Arts.

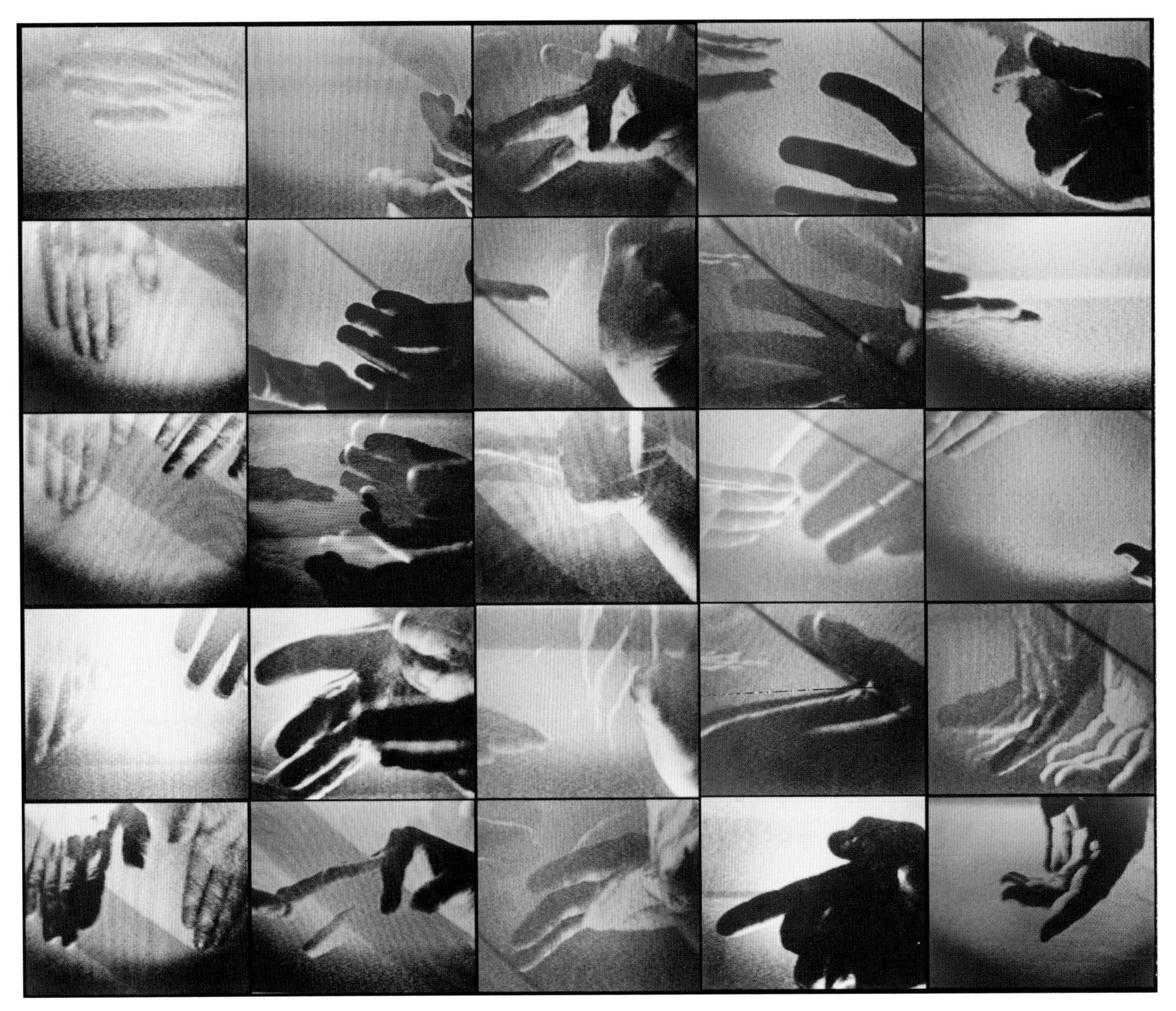

1, 2, 3, 4, 1969

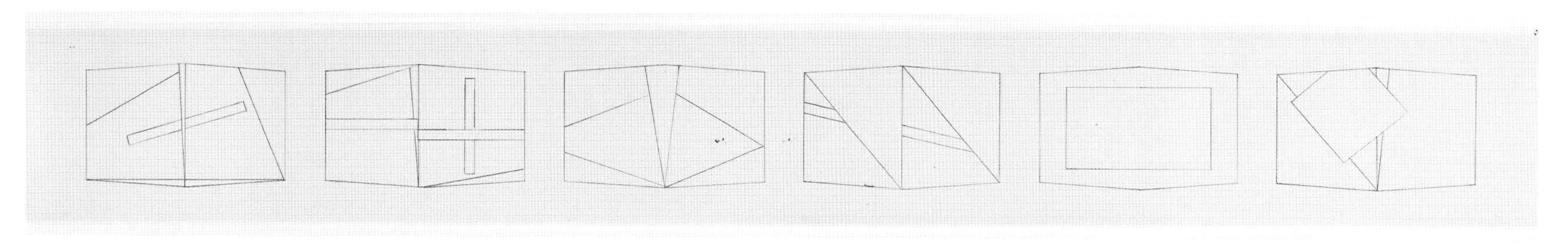

Sketches, c 1980s

Early Work

Dickie Landry's early drawings, photographs and filmic work—he didn't begin to paint until 1994—developed alongside the many artists, musicians, dancers, and performers who were challenging the Abstract Expressionist movement developed in New York in the 1950s with new approaches to all aspects of creative expression. His own artwork evolved with fundamental structures that have some element of being time-based. Repetition was a key component, and he investigated image making across media, whether through drawing on paper, still photography, film still, or moving images.

The single shape that forms the fundamental visual motif throughout Landry's artwork is the outline of an axonometric projection made by rotating an object to reveal its three dimensions. Landry refers to the tube television screens of the 1950s, the cloudy glass, slightly rounded at the corners, the shape of which he "squared off."

Fundamental to Landry's early work are ideas of randomness, harmony and repetition. Moving easily between still images, color pencil on paper, moving images, and sound, Landry's investigations were free-flowing, intuitive, and process-based.

For Landry, a roll of graph paper became a sketchbook. Idea after idea played out on the paper, some would evolve into drawings. The drawings—sometimes on paper, sometimes collage, sometimes with multiple media like videotape stills and vellum—became realized works in their simplicity and straightforwardness. Color pencil on paper created a tension of line and added a spatial dimension. Architectural vellum provided a dimension of forms, a bleeding of line, and mysterious overlays suggest images and texture.

Experimentation with the process of "rayographs"—exposing photographic paper to light without the use of a camera and then processing it normally—included the use of templates made from Chinese paper cut outs of dancers. Part of the Cibachrome paper was covered, a template was placed in the visible area, it was exposed to light, the process was repeated on the previously unexposed area, and then the print was processed. Varying exposures to light resulted in various tonal qualities on the paper.

1,2,3,4 presents an early work that captures the randomness of materials and the spirit of art-making as artists, musicians, and performers in the late 1960s and the 1970s were questioning all aspects of their disciplines; the lines between painting, music, and performance blurred. The video component of this work shows Landry's hands beating a rhythm against a piece of found foam under a pulsing light. Sound and images were recorded in one take on a Sony reel-to-reel tape deck. Placed adjacent to it is a grid of photographic stills of hands clapping—five across and five down. The work was shown in Landry's first solo exhibition at Leo Castelli Gallery in New York City. Castelli had converted a viewing area for video-based work so Landry joined the likes of Bruce Nauman, Keith Sonnier, and Lawrence Weiner in presenting his experimental videos.

Landry made the *Sound Machine* from a single pipe from a pipe organ, which emits one note with wind created by a fan in its base. The *Sound Machine* is used as a sound drone—a monotonous, continuous sound—to create an ambient backdrop for his solo saxophone concerts.

In Landry's series of still photographs, images are placed in what at first may appear as sequential, as if lifting video stills from film clips; however, the sequences may be in reverse, may be kaleidoscopic in not having a sequential order, or may highlight a specific moment when, for example, William S. Burroughs offers a seldom seen smile.

Dickie Landry, New York Stories

Dickie Landry on Philip Glass

Dickie Landry on Robert Rauschenberg

Dickie Landry on Gordon Matta-Clark

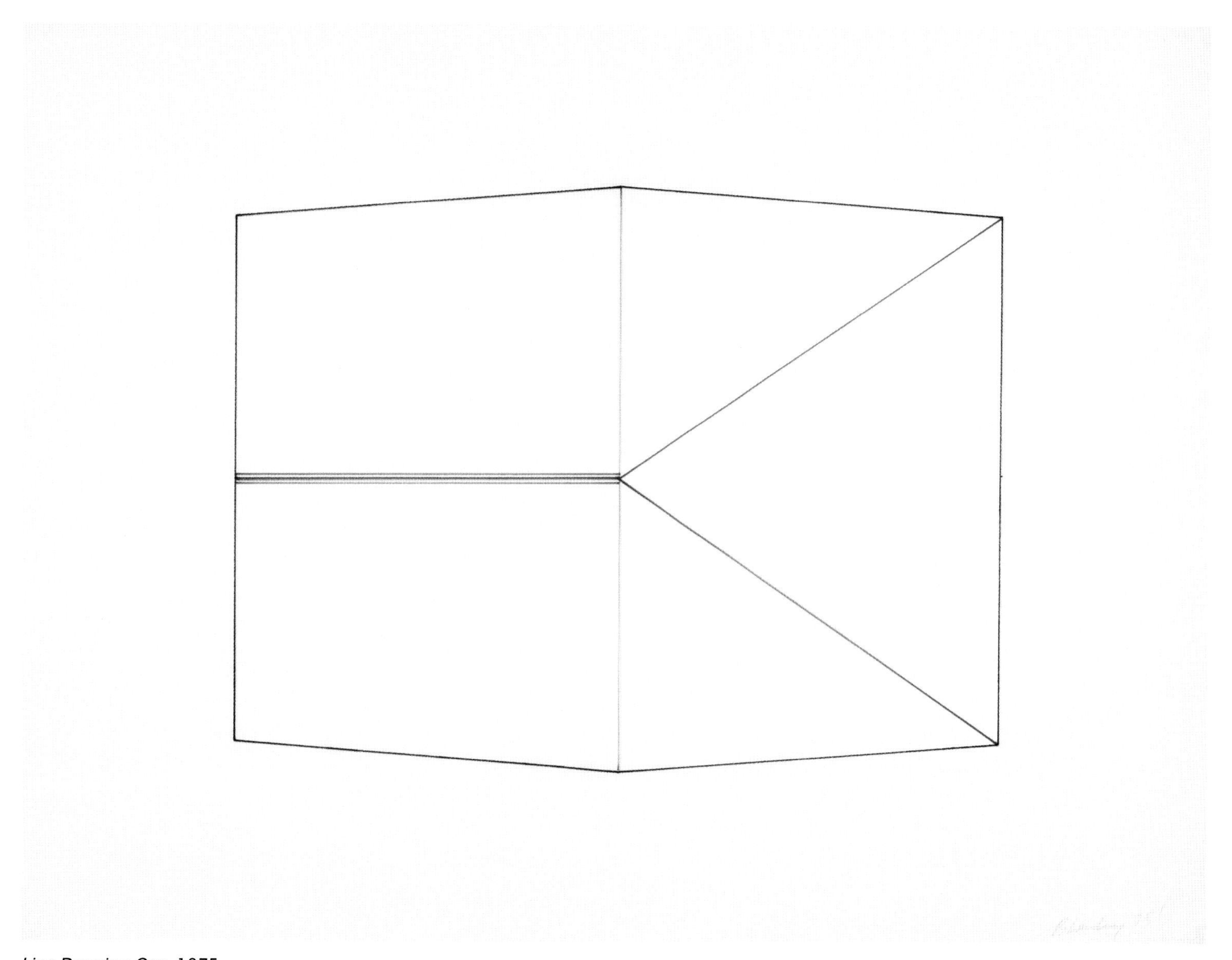

Line Drawing One, 1975

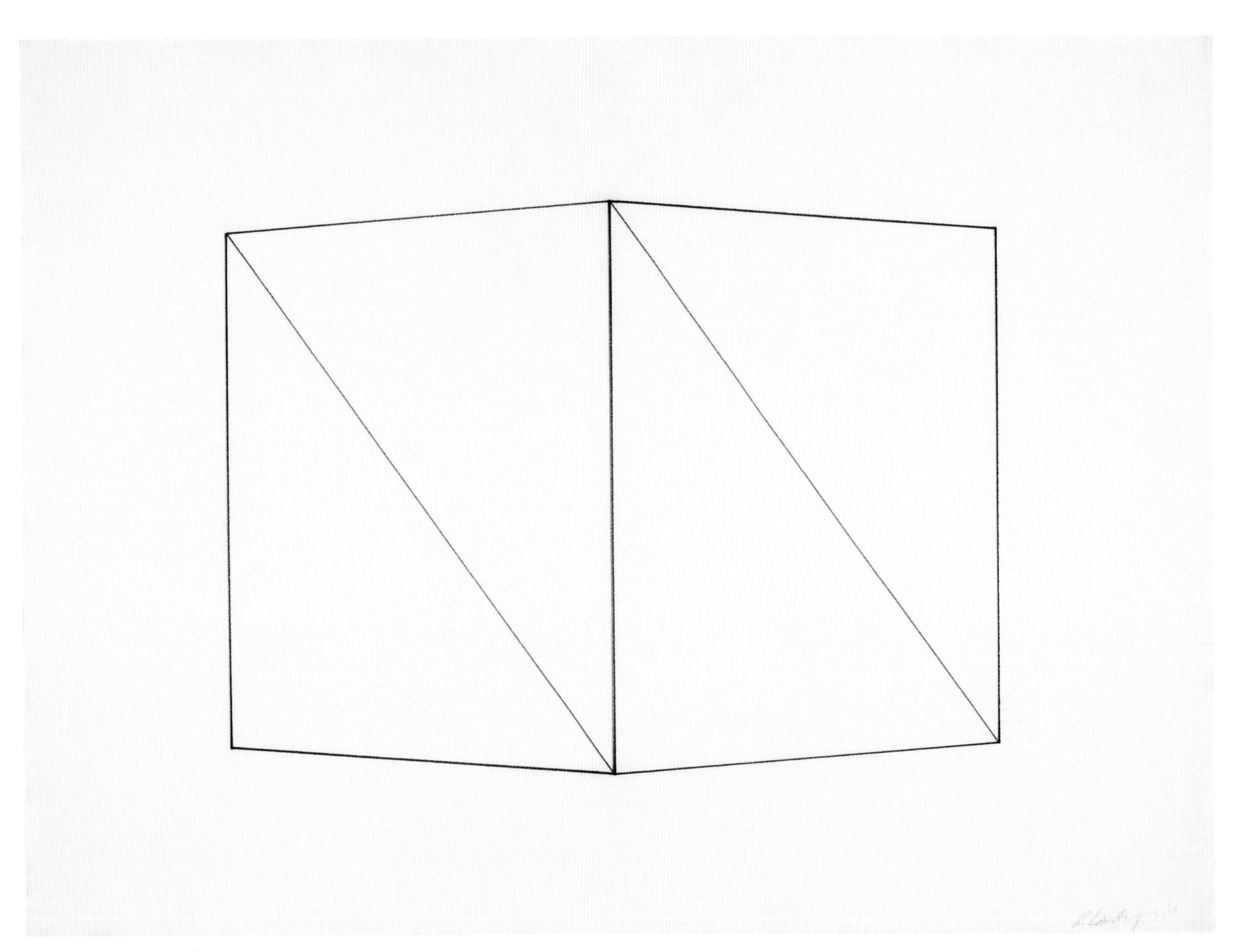

Line Drawing Two, 1975

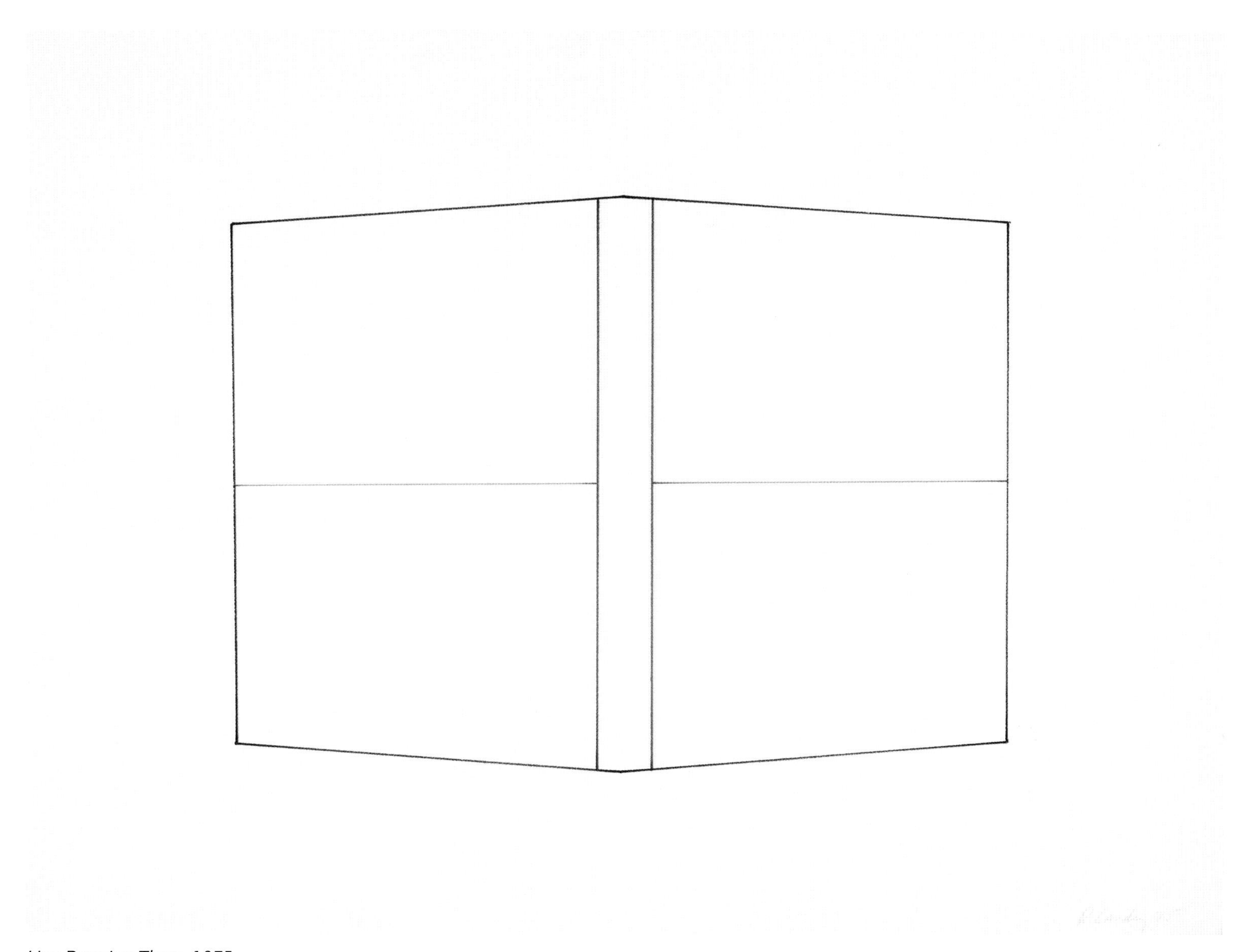

Line Drawing Three, 1975

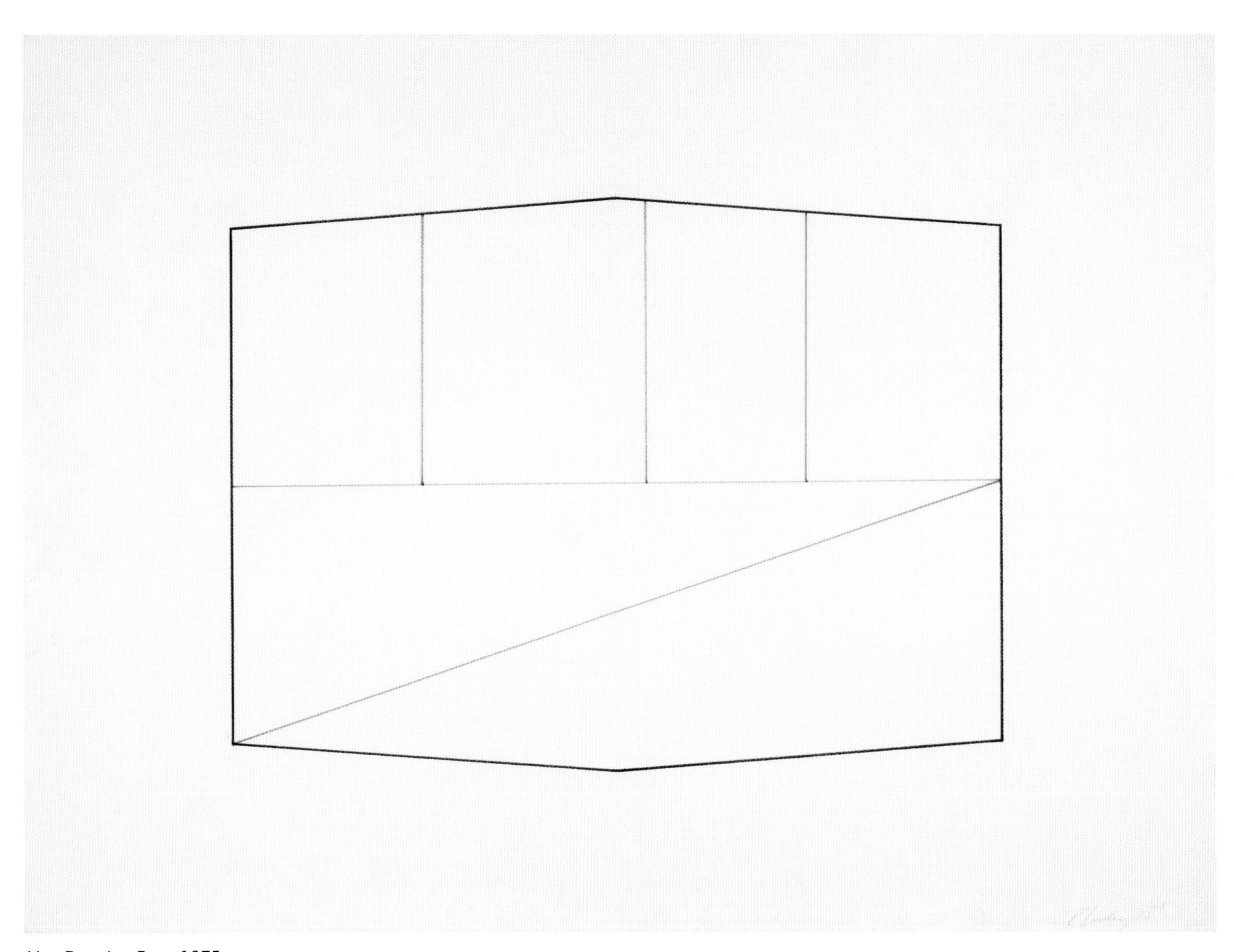

Line Drawing Four, 1975

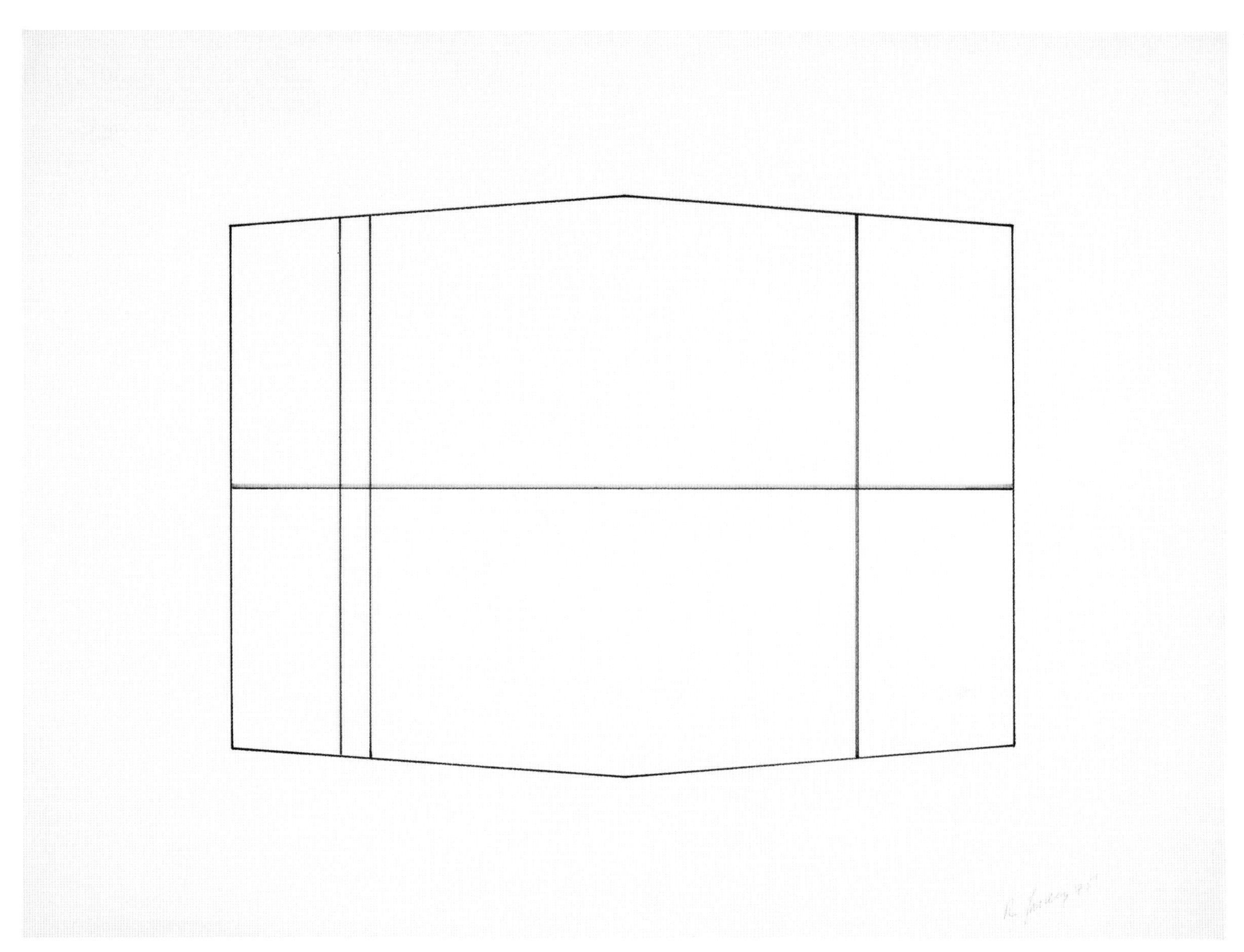

Line Drawing Five, 1975

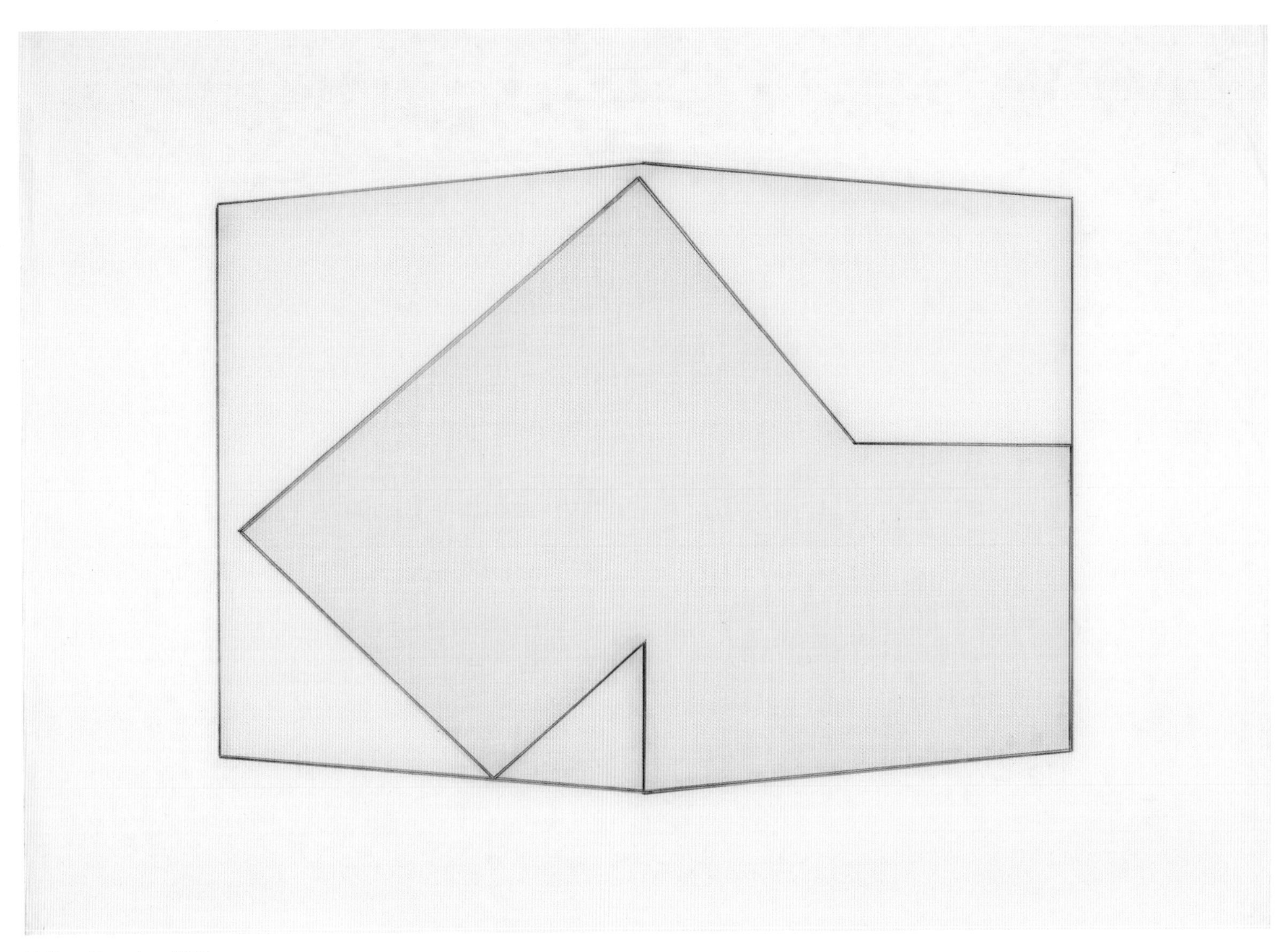

Vellum Drawing, 1971

Vellum Drawing, 1971

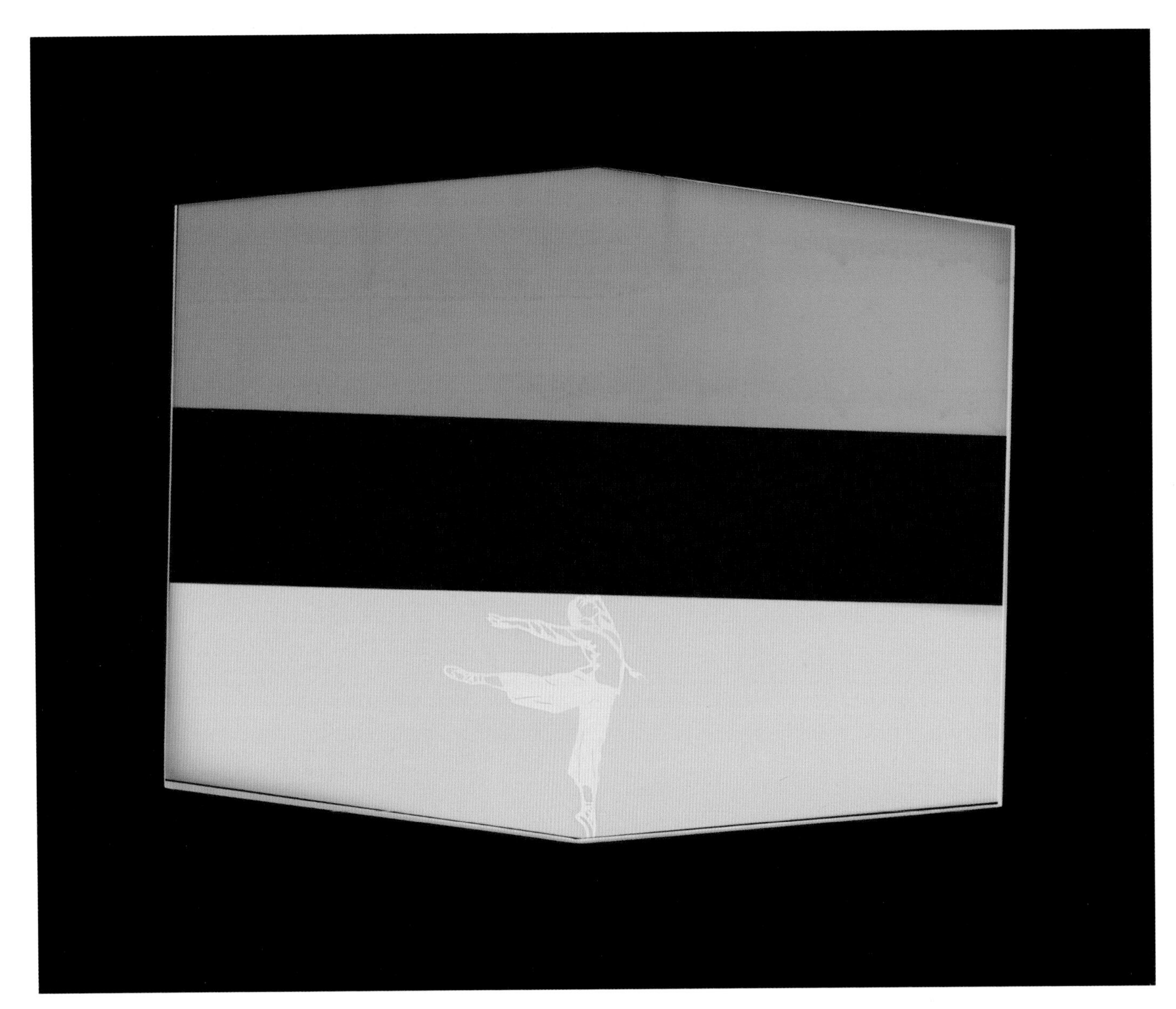

Ray o Gram, 1974

Dr. Gabe Ray o Gram, 1974

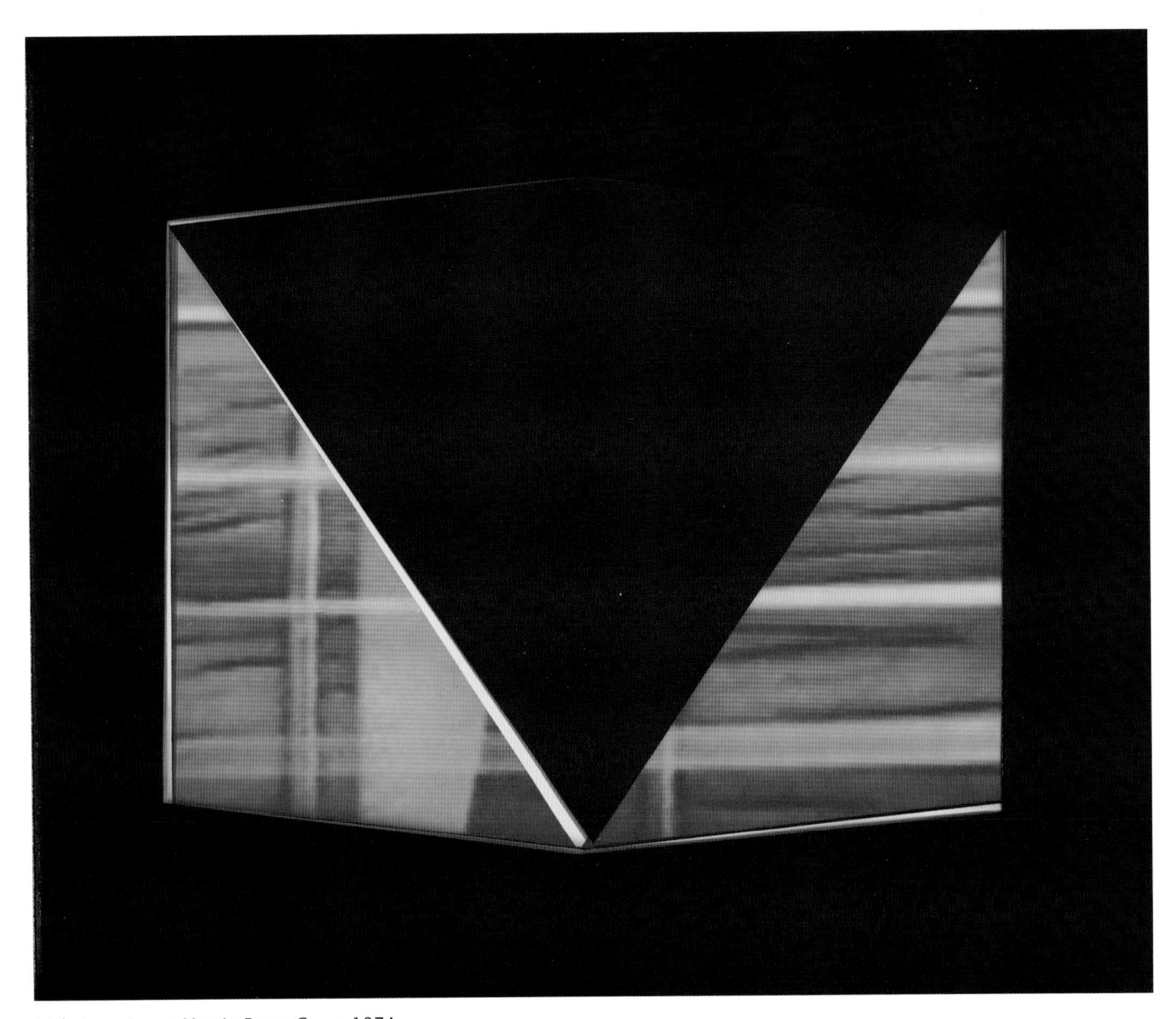

Tribute to Agnes Martin Ray o Gram, 1974

Ray o Gram, 1974

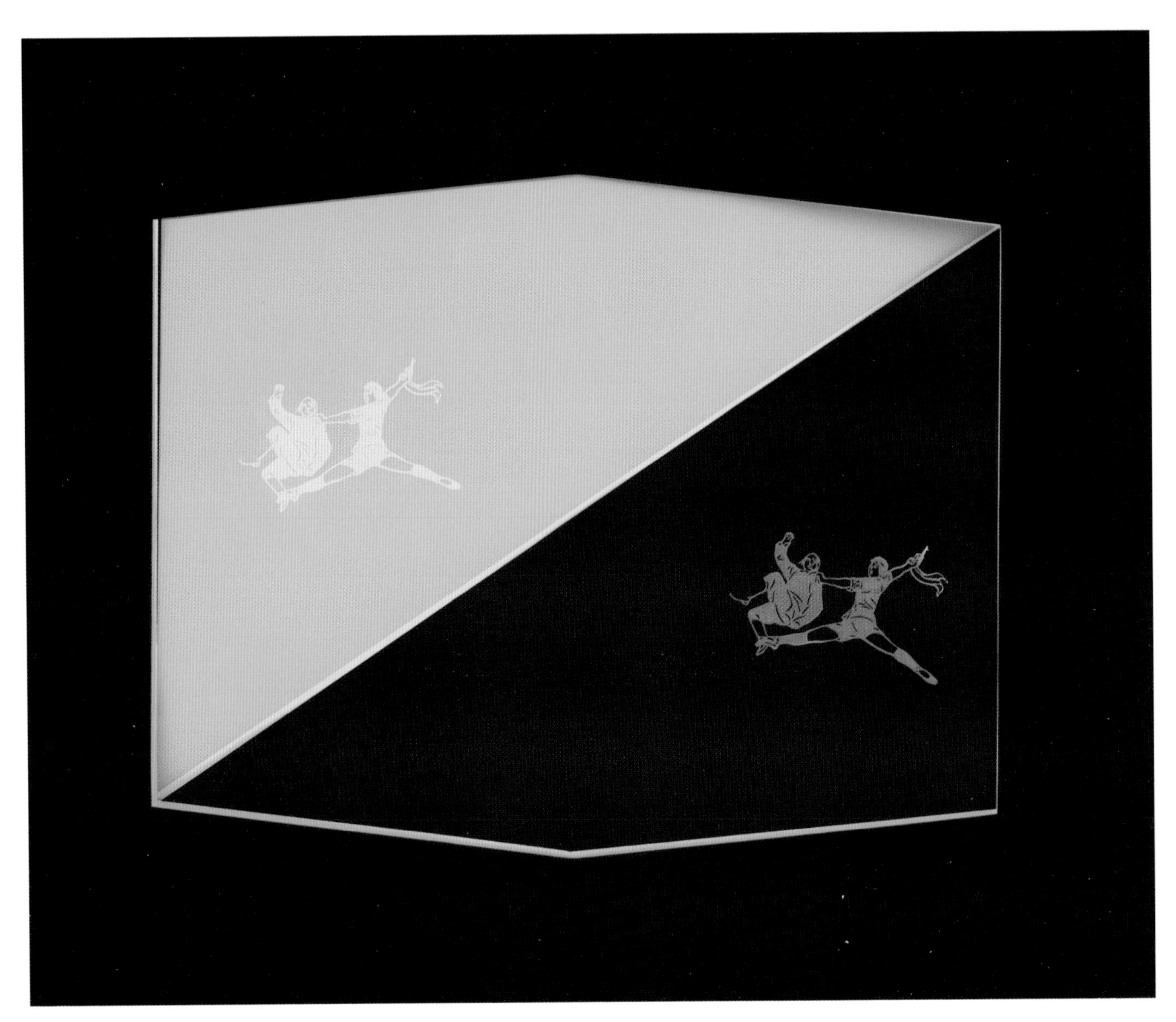

Ray o Gram, 1974

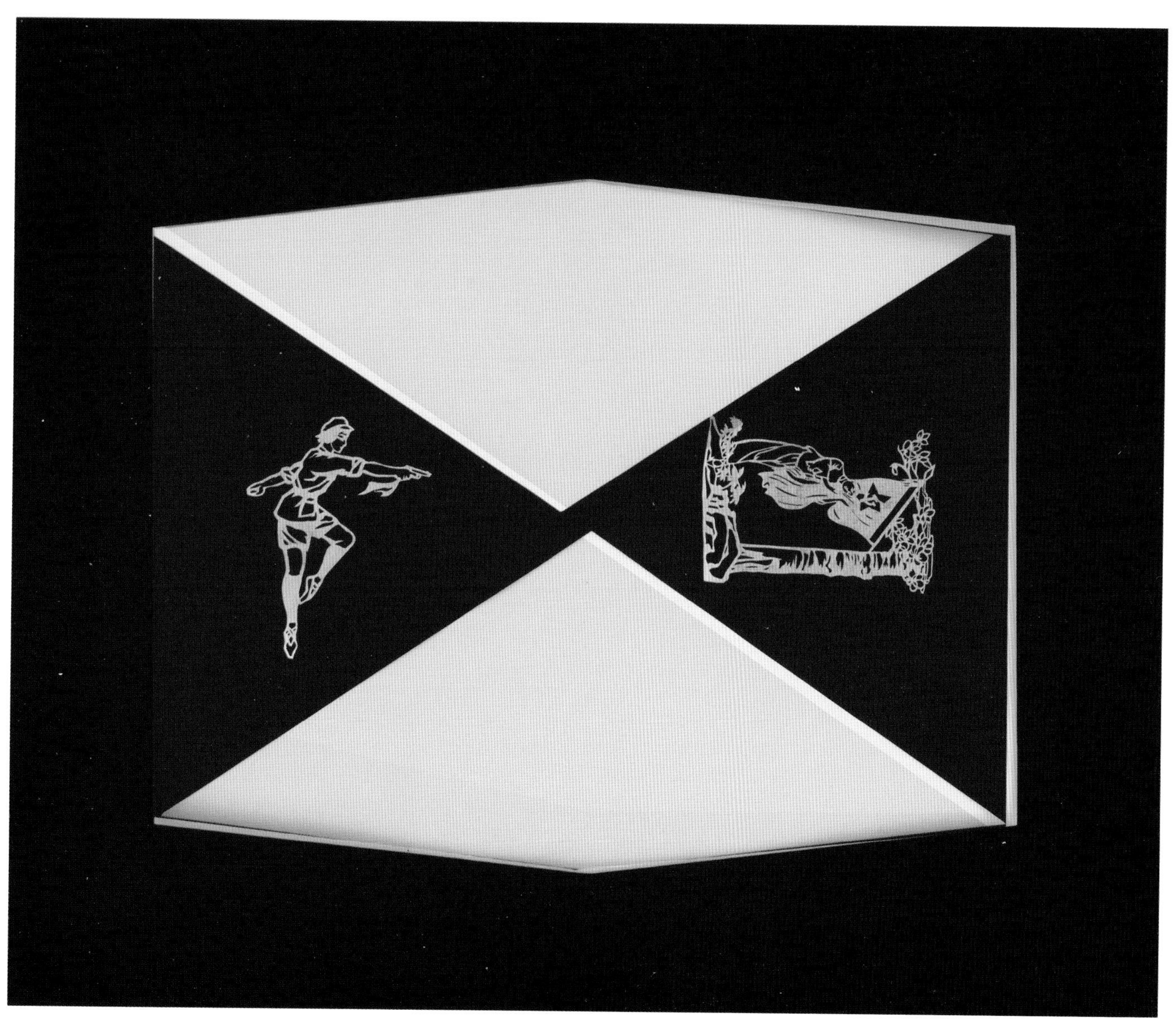

Ray o Gram, 1974

Venice Series, 1976

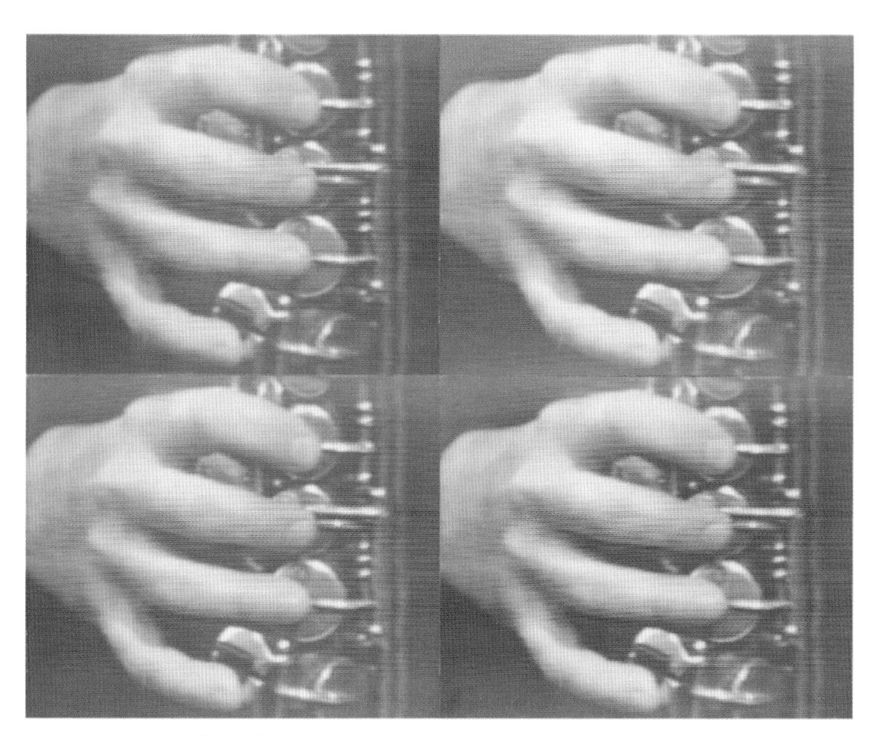

Dickie Landry, 4 Saxophones, 1972

Dickie Landry, Sax One, 1972

Dickie Landry, Divided Alto, 1972

Bruce Nauman/Philip Glass, Badminton, 1971
Richard Serra, Lead Weight, 1969

Ulrich Rückrem, Untitled, 1970

William S. Burroughs, One Smile, 1974

Dickie Landry, World Trade Center Salute, 1976

Sound Machine, 1992

Photography

Dickie Landry arrived in New York in 1969 and landed in the midst of a group of artists, composers, performers, and musicians who would radically change the direction of American Art. Responding to the abstract art of the day and its subsequent Pop Art and Minimalism movements, the artists who lived poor in the Chinese neighborhood of south Manhattan would forever change our assumptions. What is a painting? What is music? What is performance art? What is theater? Through the decade of the 1970s, Landry worked with, participated in, and documented the changing cultural perspectives expressed through the upheaval of the period.

Robert Rauschenberg had been an inspiration to the young Landry who, after seeing his 1955 combine *Bed* printed in *Time* magazine, was liberated to pursue his passion in music and art. He befriended Rauschenberg after moving to New York City and would eventually travel the world with him on his *Rauschenberg Overseas Cultural Interchange*.

Moondog was a blind musician with a long beard who dressed in a robe, a Viking helmet, patchwork pants, and who wielded a spear. He spent his days at the corner of 54th Street and Avenue of the Americas, entertaining passersby with a percussive rhythmic style that he played on drums and a portable keyboard. A cult figure from the 1950s, he is credited as a pioneer in the avant-garde minimalist music experiments of the time.

Philip Glass invented an experimental minimalist style of music and founded the Philip Glass Ensemble in 1968 to perform it. Landry was a member of the original group and worked with Glass for more than a decade. Glass has worked collaboratively with a number of artists, most notably with Robert Wilson on the opera, *Einstein on the Beach* (1976). Performed in four acts, the visual, kinetic, and musical performance revolutionized 20th century opera.

Gordon Matta-Clark, known for his temporary architectural / sculptural works created by removing sections of buildings which he documented in photography and film, introduced new and radical methods of exploring urban architecture. He was a major contributor to the growth of the avant-garde in New York which included co-founding 112 Greene Street, the seminal space for new art during the 1970s, and establishing an artist-run restaurant called Food with Caroline Gooden and Tina Girouard.

Keith Sonnier, a fellow artist from Lafayette, Louisiana, who introduced Landry to New York's new art community, experimented with sound, video, neon, transmitters, strobe lights, and performance, joined Eva Hesse, Barry Le Va, Bruce Nauman, Richard Serra, and Joel Shapiro in challenging preconceived ideas about sculpture and experimenting with industrial materials. His architectural neon wall drawings garnered world-wide attention.

Richard Serra, known for his monumental, minimalist sculpture that explores mass and space, lived and worked in New York during the 1970s. Landry was a studio assistant for four years, during which time Serra experimented with throwing molten lead into his studio walls to create casts from impact and began his exploration of balancing large plates of 1-inch thick lead in various compositions that were self-supporting.

Mabou Mines was established in New York in 1970 as an experimental theater company to explore new ideas in language, literature, music, performance art, and the visual arts. The founding group included English actor David Warrilow, an accomplished actor in works by Samuel Beckett. Early productions include *Dressed Like and Egg* (1977) and *The Lost Ones* (1977). Landry photographed their productions with music by Philip Glass.

Captiva Island, Florida Studio (Robert Rauschenberg), 1979

Glass in the Sky (Philip Glass), 1977

Moondog (Loui T. Hardin), 1969

I Love New York (Mary Heilman), 1972

Susan Rothenberg/George Trakas, 1970

Guggenheim Touch Up (Richard Serra), 1970

2+2+1, To Dickie & Tina (Richard Serra), 1969

Untitled (Bent Steel,Ulrich Rückrem), 1970

Untitled (Two Stones, Ulrich Rückrem), 1970

Untitled (Two Stones, Ulrich Rückrem), 1970

Camels (Nancy Graves Studio), 1969

Camels (Nancy Graves Studio), 1969

Suzanne Harris, Wheel, 112 Greene St, 1973

Suzanne Harris, Wheel, 112 Greene St, 1973

Brooklyn Bridge Event Pig Roast (Gordon Matta-Clark), 1971

Food (Tina Girouard, Carol Gooden, Gordon Matta-Clark), 1971

One Quart Exterior Latex Green Industrial Enamal Thown on a Brick Wall (Laurence Weiner installation with Tina Giouard), 1973

A First Quarter (Mel Kendrick, Bella Obermaier, Lawrence Weiner), 1973

Jones Beach Piece (Joan Jonas, George Trakas), 1970

Jones Beach Piece (Carolyn Gooden, Susan Rothenberg, Joan Jonas, George Trakas), 1970

Jones Beach Piece (John Erdman, Susan Rothenberg, George Trakas), 1970

Dis-Play (Keith Sonnier), 1969

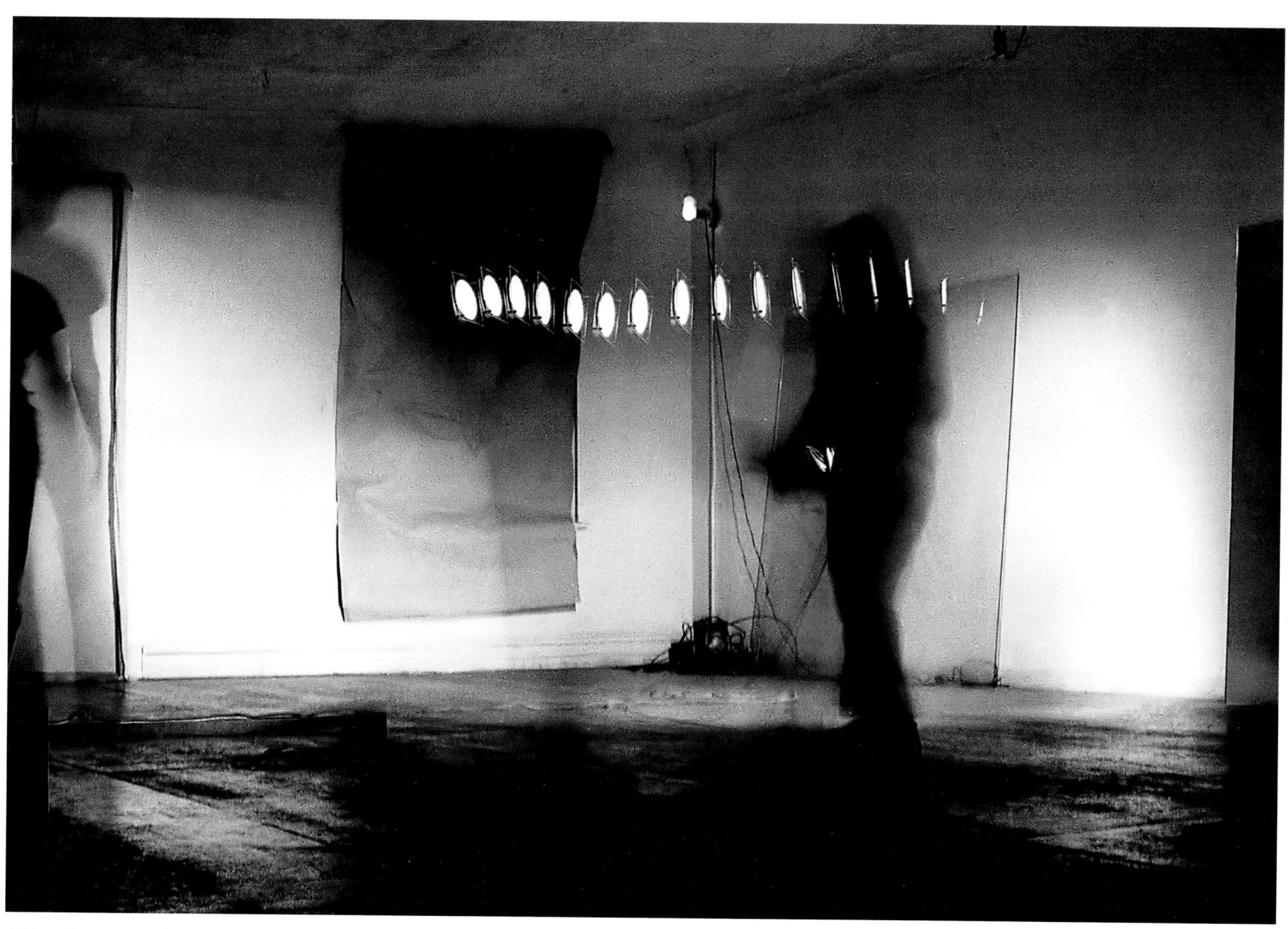

Object Situation Object (Keith Sonnier), 1969

Object Situation Object (Keith Sonnier), 1969

Four Pianos (left to right: Arthur Murphy, Philip Glass, Jon GIbson, Steve Chambers, Steve Reich), 1970

Phase Shifter Controls (Steve Riech rehearsal at Whitney Museum, NYC), 1970

Drumming (Arthur Murphy, Jon Gibson, Steve Reich, Steve Chambers rehearsing in Reich's loft), 1970

DiaLog [3], Whitney Museum of Art (Robert Wilson, Christopher Knowles, Lucinda Childs), 1976

Cycles for Pipe Organ (Jon Gibson), 1974

Samuel Beckett's Lost Ones (David Warrilow), 1975

Samuel Beckett's Lost Ones (David Warrilow), 1975

Samuel Beckett's Lost Ones (David Warrilow), 1975

Samuel Beckett's Lost Ones (David Warrilow), 1975

Dressed Like and Egg from the writings of Colette (Mabou Mines), 1976

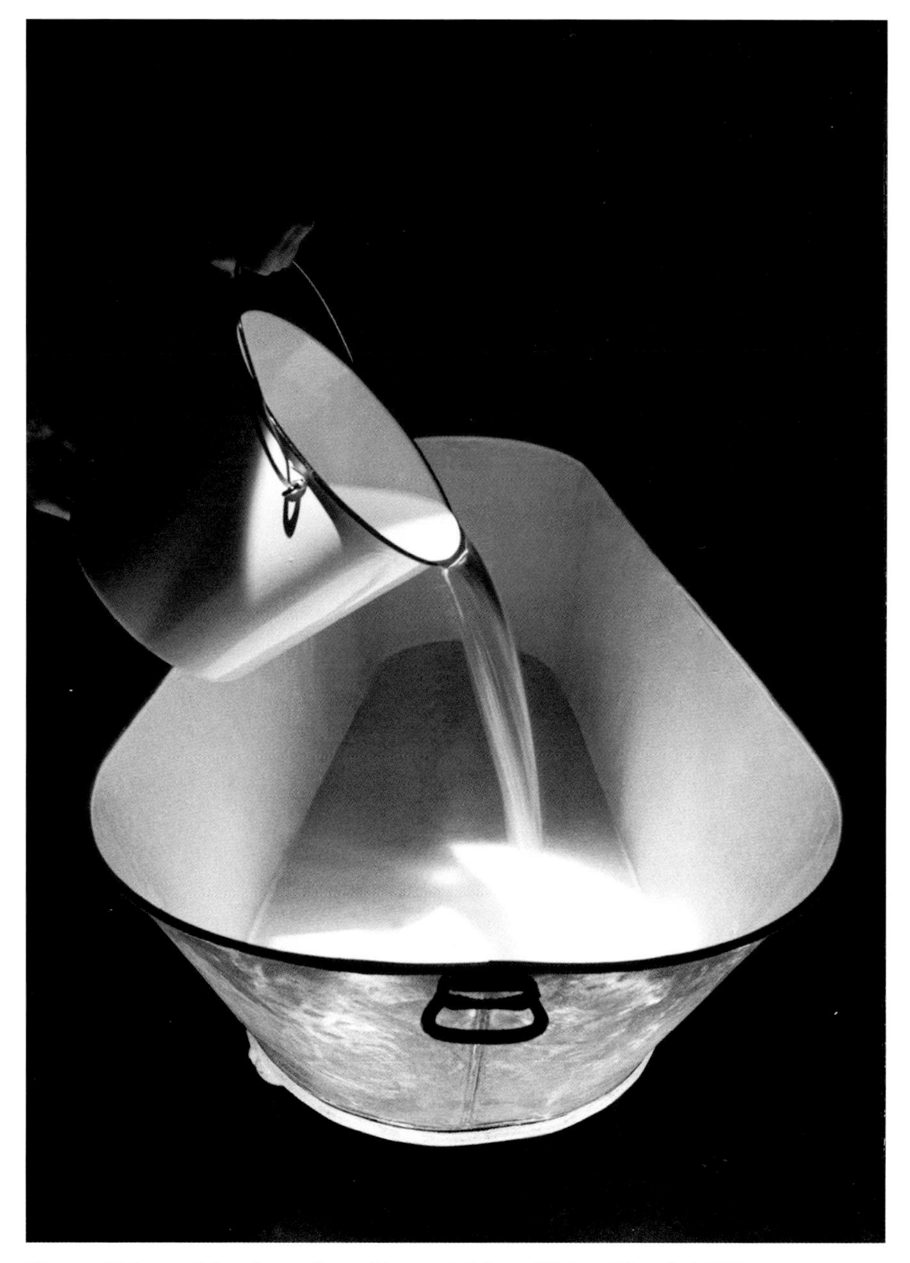

Dressed Like and Egg from the writings of Colette (Mabou Mines), 1976

Dressed Like and Egg from the writings of Colette (Mabou Mines, JoAnn Akalaitas, David Warrilow, Dog, Ellen McElduff, Ruth Maleczech), 1976

Dressed Like and Egg from the writings of Colette (Mabou Mines), 1976

Einstein on the Beach, Knee 2 (poster image for Robert Wilson/Philip Glass production), 1976

Train 1 (Robert Wilson/Philip Glass production), 1976

Trialogue Rehearsal, 1994

Trialogue score, 1994

Trialogue

Trialogue was a multidisciplinary live performance for which Dickie Landry wrote the original score. It is conceived by Landry and Babs Case as a conversation between a musician, an artist, and a dancer. The original performance premiered in 1982 at the *New York Improvisational Festival.*

For *Dickie Landry. Composer. Saxophonist. Photographer. Artist.*, the work was reset with choreography by Case, director of the Dancers' Workshop in Jackson Hole, WY, and was performed twice, once at the University of Wyoming, the other at the Jackson Hole Center for the Arts.

The university performance included four dance and two art students in the movement and visual art roles. For the Jackson Hole performance, Francesco Romo danced the movement part and Babs Case was the visual artist. Both performances included Dickie Landry as the musician.

Dickie Landry in noontime gallery walk for *Explorations in Axonometric Projections* at the Arts Association, Jackson Hole, Wyoming.

Explorations in Axonometric Projection

Dickie Landry: Explorations in Axonometric Projection focuses on Landry's work in drawing, rayographs, and painting. The single shape that forms his fundamental visual motif is the outline of an axonometric projection—a shape made from rotating an object to reveal its three dimensions, in this case a cube. Landry refers to the tube television screens of the 1950s, the cloudy glass, slightly rounded at the top and bottom shape of which he "squared off."

The earliest works on view—the "rayographs" made from exposing photographic paper to light that included the use of templates of cutout dancers—represent his earliest investigations from the 1970s. His work from the time included experiments with photography, film, and drawing between which he moved easily. His investigations were free-flowing, intuitive, and process-based.

Landry began painting in 1994. His large works are made with acrylic paint and oil stick on canvas, which enables a building up of texture. Landry's compositions create powerful, minimalistic images that play space, form, and color in a tense dialogue. More than variations on a theme, each painting is an idea unto itself, at times playful, suggestive, and unique.

Drawing Two, 1994

Drawing Three, 1994

Drawing Four, 1994

Ocana, Italy, 1994

Break Up Piece, 1995

St. Gallen, Switzerland, 1994

St. Gallen, Switzerland, 1994

Black Bar, 1995

Little Black Squares, 1995

Gold Copper Split, 2003

Rising Bed, 1995

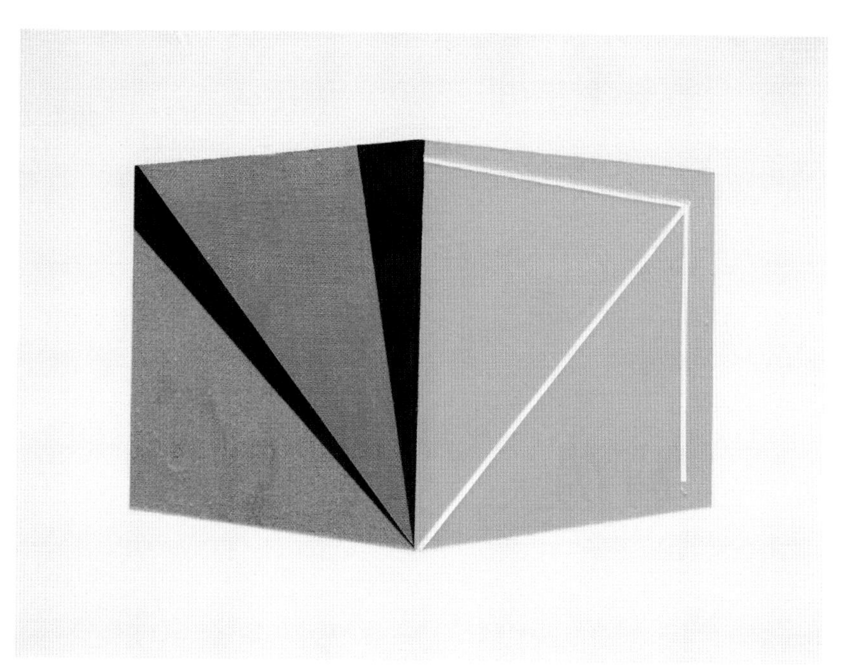

Separating Golds, 2003

Bronze With Stripe, 2003

Leaning Bronze, 1995

Black Triangle, 1995

Encaustic I, 1995

Painting

The paintings are paintings and the music is the music. They're both about individual style. When you see a Rauschenberg, a Lichtenstein or a Warhol, or hear John Coltrane or Miles Davis, you know whose work it is. I hope the same can be said of what I do.

Dickie Landry,
Paris Transatlantic Magazine
interview by Clifford Allen, August 2010

Dickie Landry made his first painting in 1994, returning to the 6-sided format of his earlier drawings and using oil stick as paint. Placed in the center of the canvas, the format becomes an object in a larger field of white. Realizing the potential of making something physical that was not a photograph, Landry pursued his large paintings, often making small sketches before committing an image to the larger canvas.

Landry describes his paintings as "three dimensions on a flat plane." His format, the flattened axonometric projection, may frame a view into another space, or contain the painting, or act as a background. His intuitive use of color, density, texture, and figure-ground are essential aspects of his minimalist works on canvas. From afar, the paintings look like oil on canvas; but on closer inspection, the beauty and unique characteristics of his preferred medium—oil stick—can be seen. In *Bed Rising* 1998, the clarity of the blue space contributes to the tension in holding the black bar suspended and creating an illusion of it rising. The densely textured *Shifted* (2001) creates a sense of mass and weight and the use of white lines suggest cuts that separate triangular segments that still complete the composition. *To the Point* (2003) uses the black background to contain a cluster of arrows that lead the eye up, around, and through the painting.

Early on, Landry envisioned incorporating photographic imagery into his canvases; however, he wasn't interested in silkscreen -- thinking it was too derivative -- or in the cumbersome chemical processes available at the time. Eventually a friend purchased a painting machine for making billboards; it was capable of painting an image in any scale onto the canvas. Through his help, Landry experimented with using photographic images in his paintings, as seen in *Are We There Yet* (2009), his first painting with an image.

Over the years, many have commented to Landry about his multiple investigations and accomplishments in visual art, composition, and music, suggesting that it is not possible to accomplish so much in one lifetime. But Landry is a true Renaissance man, cultured and deeply knowledgeable in his chosen fields as a composer, saxophonist, photographer, and artist and one who has a lifetime of accomplishments to show for it. While mostly overlooked in the art world since returning to Louisiana, he has been active internationally with his music, playing with the swamp band *Lil' Band O' Gold* (C.C. Adcock, Steve Riley, Warren Storm); played with Bob Dylan for the 2003 New Orleans Jazz & Heritage Festival; recorded with Robert Plant (Led Zeppelin) for the Fats Domino Tribute *Goin' Home* (2007); performed solo for Robert Wilson's *Grace for Grace* (1991); performed a solo concert at the Guggenheim Museum for its John Chamberlain tribute (2012); composed music for Robert Wilson's production of Jean Genet's *Le Négres* (The Blacks) in Paris (2014); performed with Laurie Anderson on *Home of the Brave* (1984) and with Paul Simon on *Graceland* (1986).

In 2014, *Dickie Landry's NYC 1969-1979,* an exhibition of photography, opened at Gallerie Anke Schmidt in Cologne, Germany, with a solo saxophone concert. The exhibition brought new light to the previously unrecognized photographs by Landry that documented the tumultuous New York scene from his unique personal perspective. That exhibition traveled to Salomon Contemporary in New York City in the spring of 2015, and forms the centerpiece of this larger survey of Landry's full artistic production at the University of Wyoming Art Museum.

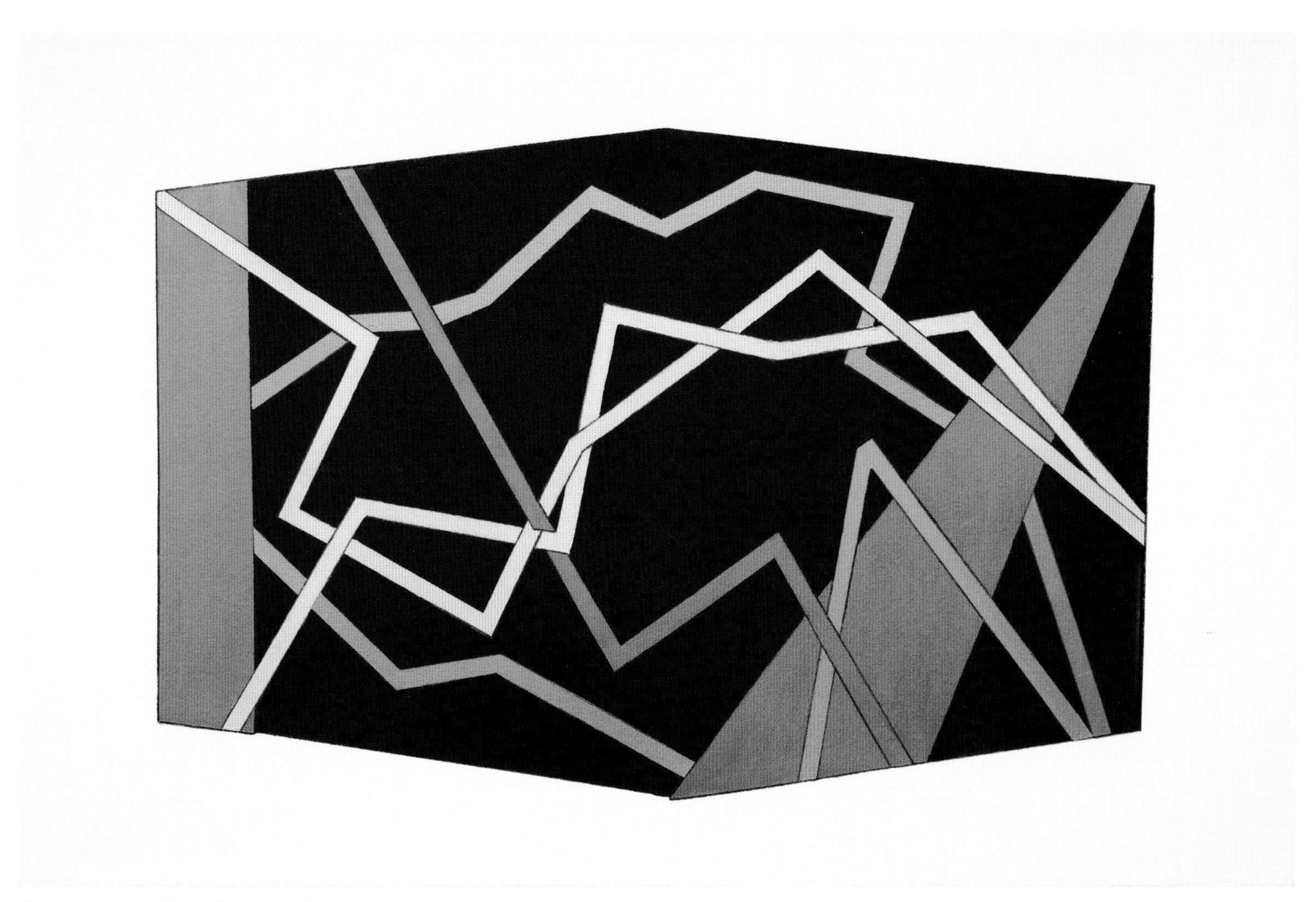

Over and Under Marrakech, 1994

Bed Rising, 1998

A, B, C, D, E, F & Z, 1994

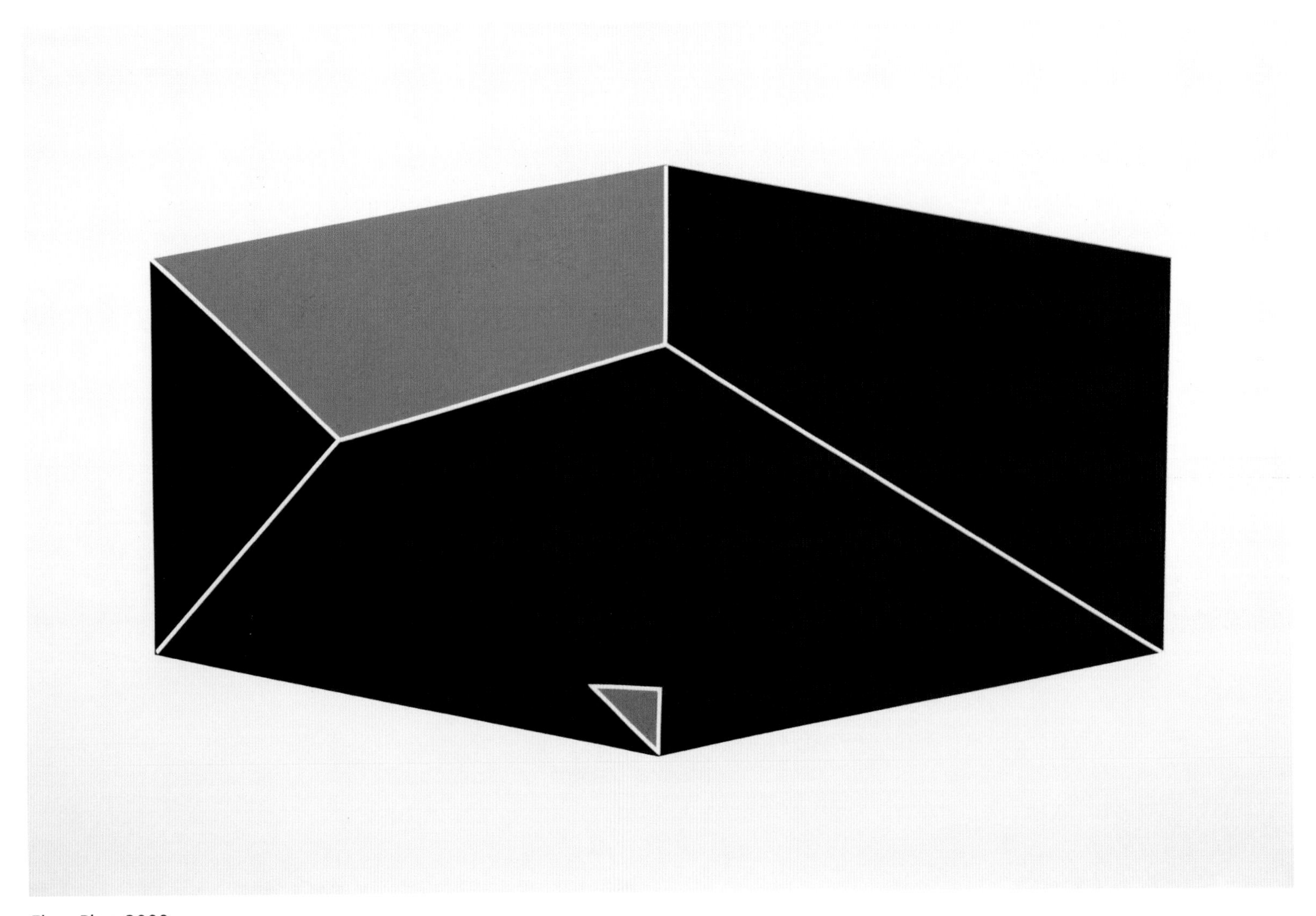

Floor Plan, 2000

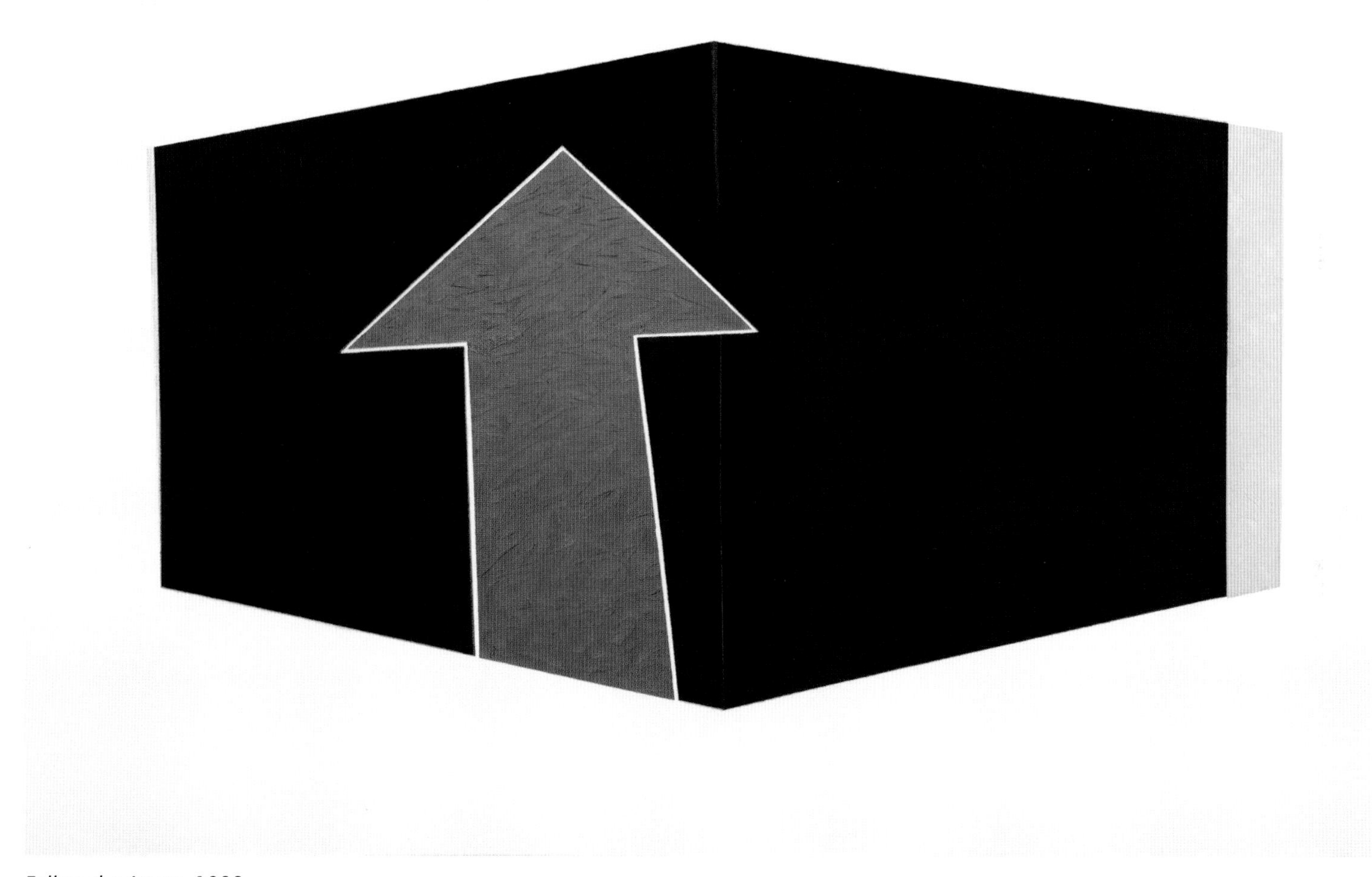

Follow the Arrow, 1998

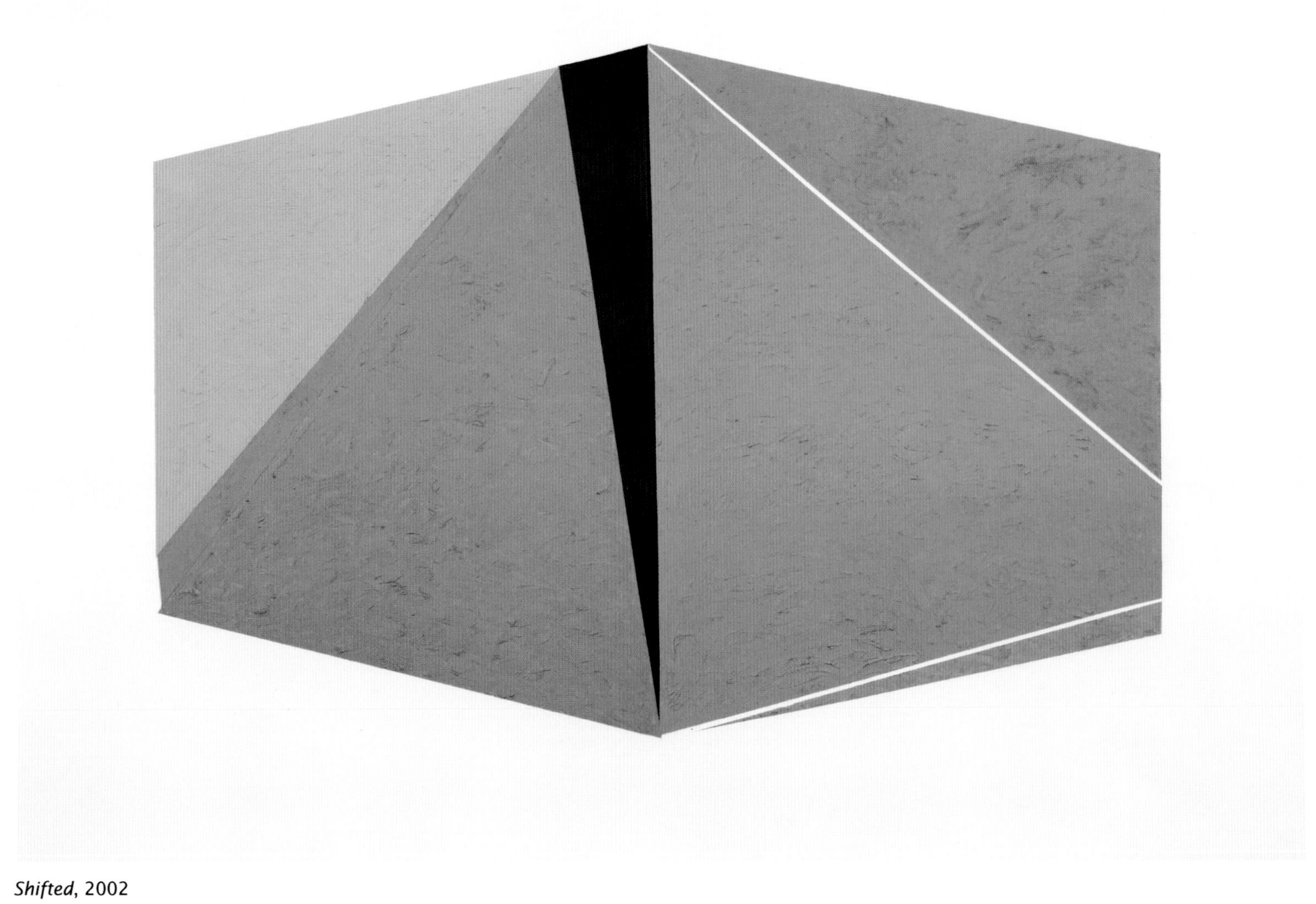

Shifted, 2002

Split Red, 2001

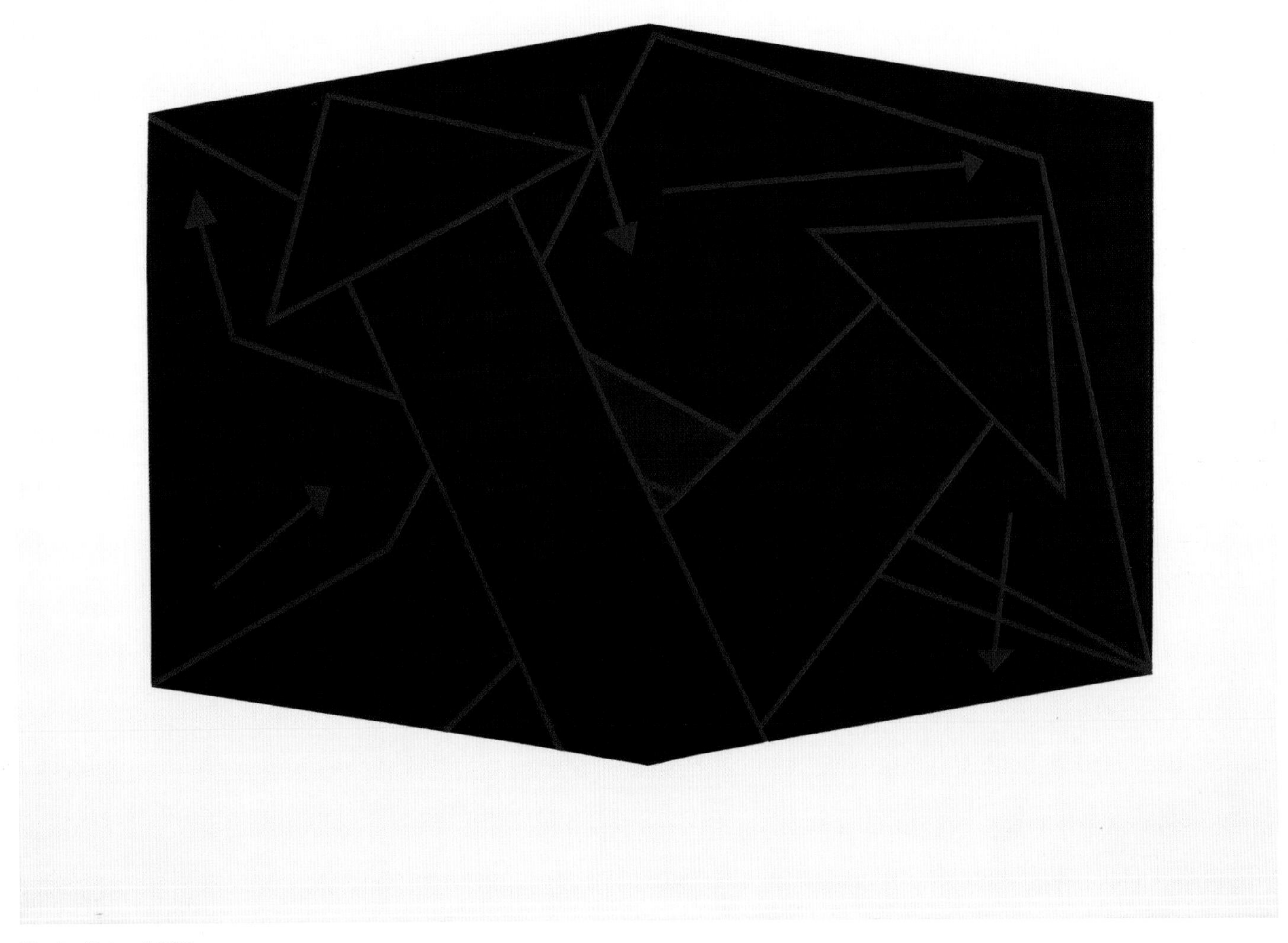

To the Point, 1996

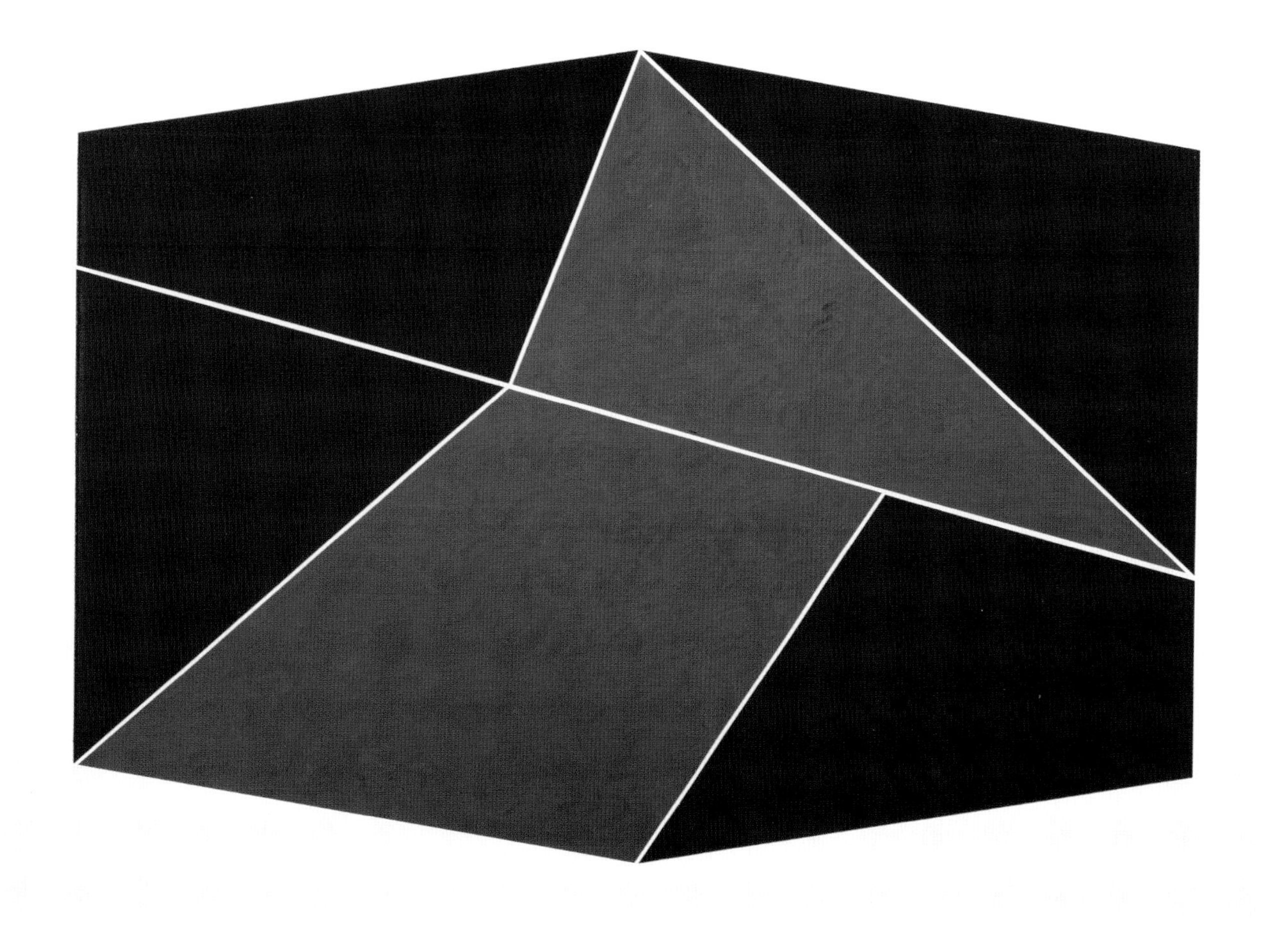

Flap, 1996

Bar Code, 1998

Black Hole, 2002

Blue Door, 2010

Dickie Landry

Composer. Saxophonist. Photographer. Artist.

Checklist
University of Wyoming Art Museum, Laramie, WY

EARLY WORK

1, 2, 3, 4, 1969, black and white photographs, 50 x 64 inches (20 x 24 each)
1, 2, 3, 4, 1969, video, variable, same size as projected
Dickie Landry, 4 Saxophones, 1972, photograph, 24 x 20 inches
Dickie Landry, Divided Alto, 1972, photograph, 9-3/8 x 11-3/4 inches
Drawing Four, 1994, color pencil on paper, 17 x 22 inches
Drawing Three, 1994, color pencil on paper, 17 x 22 inches
Line Drawing One, 1975, color pencil on paper, 24 x 32 inches
Line Drawing Two, 1975, color pencil on paper, 24 x 32 inches
Line Drawing Three, 1975, color pencil on paper, 24 x 32 inches
Line Drawing Four, 1975, color pencil on paper, 24 x 32 inches
Line Drawing Five, 1975, color pencil on paper, 24 x 32 inches
Ray o Gram, 1974, Cibachrome print, 20 x 24 inches
Ray o Gram, 1974, Cibachrome print, 20 x 24 inches
Ray o Gram, 1974, Cibachrome print, 20 x 24 inches
Score for Trialogue, 1994, graphite on paper, 11 x 32 inches
Sketches, not dated, pencil on paper, 12 x 90 inches
Sound Machine, 1992, speaker with organ tube, 14 x 14 x 51 inches
Vellum Drawing, 1971, color pencil on architectural drafting linen, photograph and color paper, 30 x 42-1/2 inches
Vellum Drawing, 1971, color pencil on architectural drafting linen, 29-3/4 x 42-1/4 inches
Venice Series, 1976, 9 black and white photographs/templates, 52 x 65 inches

PHOTOGRAPHY

2+2+1, To Dickie & Tina (Richard Serra), 1969
A First Quarter (Mel Kendrick, Bella Obermaier, Lawrence Weiner), 1973, digital print, 19 x 13 inches
Brooklyn Bridge Pig Roast (Gordon Matta-Clark), 1971, digital print, 13 x 19 inches
Bruce Nauman/Philip Glass, Badminton, 1971, digital print, 12 x 41 inches
Camels (Nancy Graves Studio), 1969, digital print, 19 x 13 inches
Camels (Nancy Graves Studio), 1969, digital print, 19 x 13 inches
Captiva Island, Florida Studio (Robert Rauschenberg), 1979, digital print, 19 x 13 inches
Cycles for Pipe Organ (Jon Gibson), 1974, digital print, 13 x 19 inches
DiaLog [3], Whitney Museum of Art (Robert Wilson, Christopher Knowles, Lucinda Childs), 1976, digital print, 13 x 19 inches
Dickie Landry, World Trade Center Salute, 1976, digital print, 16-1/2 x 11-1/4 inches
Dis-Play (Keith Sonnier), 1970, digital print, 13 x 19 inches
Dressed Like an Egg 1 from the writings of Colette (Mabou Mines), 1976, digital print, 13 x 19 inches
Dressed Like an Egg 2 from the writings of Colette (Maibou Mines), 1976, digital print, 13 x 19 inches
Dressed Like an Egg 3 from the writings of Colette (Mabou Mines), 1976, digital print, 19 x 13 inches
Dressed Like an Egg 4 from the writings of Colette (JoAnn Akalaitas, Devid Warrilow, Dog, Ellen McElduff, Ruth Maleczech), 1976, digital print, 19 x 13 inches
Drumming (Arthur Murphy, Jon Gibson, Steve Reich, Steve Chambers rehearsing in Reich's loft), 1970, digital print, 19 x 13 inches
*Einstein on the Beach, Knee 2 (*poster image for Robert WIlson/Philip Glass production), 1976, digital print, 13 x 19 inches
*Einstein on the Beach, Train 1 (*Robert WIlson/Philip Glass production, 1976, digital print), 13 x 19 inches
Food (Tina Girouard, Carol Gooden, Gordon Matta-Clark), 1971, digital print, 19 x 13 inches
Four Pianos (Steve Reich, Steve Chambers, Philip Glass, Arthur Murphy, Jon Gibson), 1970, digital print, 13 x 19 inches
Glass in the Sky (Philip Glass), 1977, digital print, 19 x 13 inches
Guggenheim Touch Up (Richard Serra), 1970, digital print, 13 x 19 inches
I Love New York (Mary Heilman), 1972, digital print, 13 x 19 inches
Jones Beach Piece (Joan Jonas and George Trakas), 1970, digital print, 13 x 19 inches
Jones Beach Piece (Carolyn Gooden, Susan Rothenberg, George Trakas), 1970, digital print, 13 x 19 inches
Jones Beach Piece (Carolyn Gooden, Susan Rothenberg, George Trakas), 1970, digital print, 13 x 19 inches
Samuel Beckett's Lost Ones (David Warrilow), 1975, digital print, 13 x 19 inches
Samuel Beckett's Lost Ones (David Warrilow), 1975, digital print, 13 x 19 inches

Samuel Beckett's Lost Ones (David Warrilow), 1975, digital print, 19 x 13 inches
Samuel Beckett's Lost Ones (David Warrilow), 1975, digital print, 13 x 19 inches
Moondog (Louis T. Hardin), 1969, digital print, 19 x 13 inches
Object Situation Object (Keith Sonnier), 1969, digital print, 13 x 19 inches
Object Situation Object (Keith Sonnier), 1969, digital print, 13 x 19 inches
One Quart Exterior Latex Green Industrial Enamel Thrown on a Brick Wall (Weiner installation with Tina Girouard), 1973, digital print, 13 x 19 inches
Phase Shifter Controls (Steve Reich rehearsal at Whitney Museum, NYC), 1970, digital print, 13 x 19 inches
Richard Serra, Lead Weight, 1969, digital print, 12 x 41 inches
Self-Portrait, 1969, digital print, 19 x 13 inches
Susan Rothenberg / George Trakas, 1970, digital print, 13 x 19 inches
Trialogue Rehearsal, 1994, silver gelatin, 10 x 8 inches, lent by Babs Case
Ulrich Ruckrem, Strip 13, 1970, digital print, 11-1/4 x 40-1/2 inches
Untitled (Two Stones, Ulrich Rückrem), 1970, digital print, 13 x 19 inches
Untitled (Two Stones, Ulrich Rückrem), 1970, digital print, 13 x 19 inches
Wheel (Suzanne Harris), 1973, digital print, 13 x 19 inches
Wheel (Suzanne Harris), 1973, digital print, 13 x 19 inches
William S. Burroughs, One Smile, 1974, digital print, 21-1/2 x 41 inches

PAINTING

A, B, C, D, E, F, & Z, 1994, oil and acrylic on canvas, 63 x 100 inches
Are We There Yet?, 2001, oil, acrylic, and ink on canvas, 32 x 51 inches
Bed Rising, 1998, oil and acrylic on canvas, 35 x 54 inches
Black Bar, 1995, acrylic on canvas, 9 x 12 inches
Blue Door, 2010, oil and acrylic on canvas, 52 x 76 inches
Blue to the Edge, 1994, oil and acrylic on canvas, 42 x 66 inches
Floor Plan, 2000, oil and acrylic on canvas, 52 x 72 inches
Leaning Bronze, 1995, acrylic on canvas, 11 x 14 inches
Little Black Squares, 1995, acrylic on canvas, 11 x 14 inches
Shifted, 2002, oil and acrylic on canvas, 52 x 72 inches
Split Red, 2001, oil and acrylic on canvas, 48 x 68 inches
To The Point, 1996, oil and acrylic on canvas, 52 x 78 inches

All objects lent by the artist unless otherwise noted.

Dickie Landry

Explorations in Axonometric Projections

Checklist
Center for the Arts, Jackson Hole, WY

Bar Code, 1998, oil and acrylic on canvas, 52 x 78 inches
Air Space, 2000, oil and acrylic on canvas, 52 x 64 inches
Over and Under Marrakech, 1994, acrylic on canvas, 36 x 54 inches
Diamonds in Hand, 2008, oil and acrylic on canvas, 54 x 79 inches
Flap, 1996, oil and acrylic on canvas, 52 x 78 inches
Black Hole, 2002, oil and acrylic on canvas, 52 x 72 inches
Follow the Arrow, 1998, oil and acrylic on canvas, 52 x 78 inches
Ocana, Italy, 1994, color pencil on paper, 15 x 18 inches
Ocana, 1994, pencil on paper, 15 x 18 inches
Drawing Two, 1994, color pencil on paper, 17 x 22 inches
St. Gallen, Switzerland, 1994, pencil on paper, 15 x 18 inches
Break Up Piece, 1995, pencil on paper, 15 x 18 inches
Encaustic 1, 1995, acrylic on canvas, 12 x 16 inches
Photograph with Poetry, 2002, black and white photograph/template, 20 x 24 inches
Tribute To Agnes Martin Ray O Gram, 1974, Cibachrome print, 20 x 24 inches
Dr. Gabe Ray o Gram, 1974, Cibachrome print, 20 x 24 inches
Gold Copper Split, 2003, colored pencil on paper, 16 x 20 inches
Bronze With Stripe, 2003, acrylic on canvas, 11 x 14 inches
Separating Golds, 2006, acrylic on canvas, 11 x 14 inches
Rising Bed, 1995, acrylic on canvas, 11 x 14 inches
Black Triangle, 1995, acrylic on canvas, 11 x 14 inches

Richard "Dickie" Landry

Born in Cecilia, Louisiana in 1938, Landry began his musical training at the age of six when he joined the St. Joseph Catholic Church Choir singing Gregorian Chant seven days a week for six years. Landry picked up the saxophone at age ten and continued the journey that would take him places far removed from the small town in St. Martin Parish where he was raised. After attending what is presently known as the University of Louisiana at Lafayette where he majored in music education, Landry taught for two years in the rural community of Chataignier in Evangeline Parish. Restless and tired of playing in a blue-eyed soul band, The Swing Kings, in 1969 Landry moved to New York City to broaden his musical horizons and find work.

The avant-garde art scene in New York City was about to explode after a period of Abstract Expressionism and Pop Art. Landry soon fell in with a crowd of artists, musicians, dancers and theater people that included Keith Sonnier, Robert Rauschenberg, Gordon Matta-Clark, Robert Smithson, Michael Heizer, Walter de Maria, Steve Reich, Philip Glass, Laurie Anderson, Susan Rothenberg, Nancy Graves, Spalding Gray, Joan Jonas, Richard Serra, Mabou Mines, Chuck Close, Robert Wilson, Lawrence Weiner, Joseph Kosuth, Bruce Nauman, Trisha Brown, Deborah Hay, Mary Heilmann, and others who are now considered visionaries in their respective fields. It was at this time that Landry took up photography, not as an art form but simply to supplement his income. When not playing music, he would be hired by his newfound artist friends to help with their performances, installations, and exhibits. He would ask if he could take pictures, not thinking of documenting anything - it was just a way to make extra money. He took his camera everywhere and became quite proficient at printing, using the same intense focus he would also apply to his music. Little did he know all these years later that he would amass a singular collection of photographs that would document the New York art scene of the 1970s from a unique insider's perspective.

Landry's first concert in New York City was in 1972 at the Leo Castelli Gallery with a group of expatriates from Louisiana. That same year he began presenting his work in solo concerts on tenor saxophone, pioneering the use of a quadraphonic delay system that allowed him to form a live quintet of his own voicing (his original sound plus four timed delayed repeats). Since then he has given concerts in the United States, Europe, Canada, Mexico, Russia, Cuba, Haiti, Japan, South America, Taiwan, and India. The most noteworthy of these concerts include the Festival d'Automne, Paris; Centre d'Art Contemporain, Geneva; Stedelijk Museum, Amsterdam; Palais de Beaux Arts, Brussels; Stadlijk Museum, Munich; Sao Bento Cathedral, Sao Paulo; The Retreat, Ahmedabad, India; and the Rufino Tamayo Museum, Mexico City.

In the United States Landry has performed in major concert halls, art galleries, museums, universities, and churches. The list includes: Carnegie Hall, Town Hall, The Kitchen, Metropolitan Opera House, Cathedral of St. John the Divine, Leo Castelli Gallery, Whitney Museum, Guggenheim Museum, Museum of Modern Art, National Gallery, Washington, D.C., as well as the Next Wave Festival at the Brooklyn Academy of Music in New York City. Landry often performs in the South including New Orleans Museum of Art, Contemporary Art Center, and New Orleans Jazz Festival in Louisiana, and in Houston, Texas at The Fine Arts Museum, Rice University, Rothko Chapel, Contemporary Art Museum, and The New Music America Festival in Houston and in Miami, Florida.

In addition to Landry's solo career, he has collaborated with other composers, artists and choreographers. In 1969 he was a founding member of the original group that formed the Philip Glass Ensemble and performed with the ensemble until 1981. He was on all concerts, tours, and recordings of that period including *Einstein on the Beach,* an opera by Robert Wilson and Glass, which is widely credited as one of the greatest artistic achievements of the 20th century. He has also worked with David Byrne and the Talking Heads on the *Speaking in Tongues (Slippery People)* album for which he received a Gold Record Award. In 1984 Landry began collaboration with Laurie Anderson at the Next Wave Festival in *Set/Reset* with choreographer Trisha Brown and artist Robert Rauschenberg. This collaboration continued with his inclusion in Anderson's *Mister Heartbreak* tour of America and Japan. These efforts culminated in the feature film production of *Home of the Brave* and the CD of the same name. Landry has collaborated with artists Keith Sonnier, Lawrence Weiner, Chuck Close and Richard Serra and received commissioned works from choreographers Babs Case, Trisha Brown, Deborah Hay, and Jane Comfort.

In 1986 Landry invited Paul Simon to Louisiana to work with local Zydeco musicians. This collaboration resulted in the song *That Was Your Mother* on the album *Graceland* for which Landry was awarded a Gold and Multi-Platinum sales award record. Recently Landry collaborated with the successful Lafayette-based rock band *Givers* performing the Simon song for the upcoming 25th anniversary tribute to the album *Graceland.*

Dominique de Menil commissioned "Mass for Pentecost Sunday" a Catholic Mass in Latin for the opening of The Menil Collection in Houston, Texas. The Mass was premiered at the Rothko Chapel June 1987.

Landry has performed in Mexico, Cuba, Russia and the National Gallery in Washington, D.C. for the openings of *Rauschenberg's Overseas Cultural Interchange* (*ROCI*) world exhibition tour. He also performed at many of Rauschenberg's gallery and museum openings. In 2009, Landry performed for Robert Rauschenberg's Memorial Services in Fort Myers, Florida, the Aratani/Japan American Theatre in Los Angeles, and the Metropolitan Museum Egyptian Room in New York City.

After moving back to Louisiana in 1995, Landry, along with C.C. Adcock and Steve Riley, formed an all-star Swamp-Pop band called Lil' Band O' Gold, with legendary

Swamp-Pop singer and drummer, Warren Storm. The band is still performing, with tours of the U.S., England, New Zealand and Australia under their belts. At the 2003 New Orleans Jazz & Heritage Festival, Bob Dylan invited Landry to play with the band for the two and half hour set. In May 2007, Landry recorded two songs along with Lil Band O' Gold with Robert Plant (Led Zeppelin) for *Goin' Home,* a Fats Domino Tribute two CD set. Landry performed with Zydeco musician Terrance Simien at the 2008 Grammy Awards in Los Angeles, where Simien walked away with the first ever Zydeco / Cajun Grammy. In 2014, Terrance received his second Grammy. Landry acted as manager for the first five years of Simien's career.

Landry performed his *Solo* for Robert Wilson's production of *Grace for Grace* at The Cathedral of St. John the Divine in New York City in 1991. The years 2009 and 2010 found Landry working with Robert Wilson, Ornette Coleman, Mei-Yun Tang and the U Theatre from Taipei on a musical theatre production inspired by the story of Admiral Zheng He, which portrays the travels of this 15th century Chinese navigator and explorer. *1433, The Grand Voyage* opened Feb. 20th, 2010 as part of the Taiwan International Festival at the National Theatre in Taipei.

In 2012, Landry performed a *Solo* concert in tribute to the late sculptor John Chamberlain at the Guggenheim Museum in New York City. At the same time he had an exhibition of his artwork at the Salomon Contemporary Gallery. Lil Band O' Gold opened for Robert Plant's summer 2013 southern tour.

At age 75, Landry composed music for Robert Wilson's 2014 production of *Le Nègres*, (The Blacks), A Clown Show by Jean Genet. The six-week performance sold out and toured France after its Paris run.

Landry's exhibition *Dickie Landry's NYC 1969-1979* opened at the Gallerie Anke Schmidt Gallery in Cologne, Germany, in September with a solo concert. The exhibit then opened at the Salomon Contemporary Gallery in New York City on Feb. 26, 2015 and the University of Wyoming at Laramie September and at the Center for the Arts in Jackson, Wyoming, 2015.

2016 finds Dickie Landry's first painting exhibit at Fort Gansevoort Gallery in New York.

Besides all of the above, Landry also has been managing his 80-acre pecan farm for 40 years, and might add that he does it alone...

Dickie Landry

Composer. Saxophonist. Photographer. Producer. Artist

PROFESSIONAL EXPERIENCE

Solo Concerts, 1972 - present: United States, Germany, Switzerland, Austria, France, Spain, Italy, England, Netherlands, Belgium, Yugoslavia, Canada, Mexico, Russia, Cuba, Haiti, Brazil, India, Japan, Taiwan

Philip Glass, *Ensemble*, 1969 -1981

Robert Wilson, *Einstein on the Beach*, 1976

Talking Heads, *Speaking in Tongues*, 1983, Gold Record

Laurie Anderson, *Home of the Brave* - Heartbreak Tour & Film, 1984

Paul Simon, *Graceland,* 1986, Gold and Platinum Record

Robert Wilson, *Grace for Grace,* 1991

Bob Dylan, *New Orleans Jazz Festival,* 2003

Lil Band O' Gold, *Swamp Pop,* 2004/2014

True Man Posse, *Creole Reggae*, 2006

Robert Plant, *Going Home*, Tribute CD to Fats Domino, 2007

Robert Wilson, *1433*, 2010

Guggenheim Museum, 2012

Robert Wilson, *The Blacks*, 2014

SELECTED RECORDINGS

Music with Changing Parts, 1970, with Philip Glass

Similar Motion, 1971, with Philip Glass

Music in Twelve Parts (Parts 1 & 2), 1974, with Philip Glass

North Star, 1975, with Philip Glass

Music in Fifths, 1975, with Philip Glass

Einstein on the Beach, 1976, with Philip Glass

Solos, 1972, Richard Landry

Four Cuts Placed In, 1973, Richard Landry

Having Been Built On Sand, 1974, Richard Landry/Lawrence Weiner

Fifteen Saxophones, 1977, Richard Landry

Speaking in Tongues, 1983, with Talking Heads

Innocent, 1984, with Peter Gordon

These Things Happen, 1984, with David van Teighem

Causal Gods, 1986, with Jerry Harrison

Home of the Brave, 1984, with Laurie Anderson

Graceland, 1986, with Paul Simon

Safety in Numbers, 1987, with David van Teighem

Lil Band O' Gold, 2002, with Warren Storm, C.C. Adcock, and Steve Reily

Creole Reggae, 2003, with True Man Posse

Frigg A Go Go, 2003, with Frigg

Goin' Home, 2007, Robert Plant/Lil Band o' Gold 2007 Fats Domino Tribute

Solo, 2007, Dickie Landry

Lil Band o' Gold, 2010

PRODUCER

Tribute to the Blues, 1978, Carnegie Hall with Clifton Chenier, John Lee Hooker, Lighting Hopkins, Honeyboy Edwards, Big Mama Thorton, and Lighting Slim

Zydeco on the Bayou, CD, 1991, Terrance Simien & the Mallet Playboys (Zydeco)

Blue Dog, CD, 1992, John DuBois (Cajun)

FILMS

Home of the Brave, Laurie Anderson, Director

The Big Easy, Jim McBride, Director

Four Cuts Placed In, Lawrence Weiner, Director

A First Quarter, Lawrence Weiner, Director

Office Baroque, Gordon Matta-Clark

New Orleans Mon Amour, Michael Almereyda, Director

Slow Pan For Bob, Chuck Close

VIDEOS (SELECTED)

Distributed by Video Data Bank, Chicago Institute of the Arts

1,2,3,4

Quad Suite

Sax One

Divided Alto

COMMISSIONS (SELECTED)

Mass for Pentecost Sunday, Dominique de Ménil & Ménil Foundation Commission for the inaugural opening of the Ménil Collection, Houston, Texas

Premier, Rothko Chapel, Houston, Texas, 1987

New Music America Festival, Miami, Florida, 1988

Abbey de Slyvannes Cameras, France, 1988

Yale School of Sacred Music New Haven, CT, 1989

Sao Bento Cathedral, Sao Paulo, Brazil

New Music Festival, Madrid, Spain 1998

Voix Sacrèes du Monde (Sacred Music Festival), Lausanne, Switzerland 1999

ROCI (Rauschenberg Overseas Cultural Interchange), performed as a soloist with the exhibition tour of the works of Robert Rauschenberg:

Rufino Tamayo Museum, Mexico City, Mexico

Tretyakov Gallery, Moscow, Russia,

Museo Nacional de Bellas Artes, Havana, Cuba

Castillo de la Fuerza, Havana, Cuba

Casa de las Americas, Havana, Cuba

National Gallery, Washington D.C.

Astral Convertible, Trisha Brown Dance Company, Robert Rauschenberg sets. Premiered City Center, New York City and the Montpellier Dance Festival, France

DANCE

Astral Convertible, Trisha Brown Dance Company/Sets Robert Rauscenberg

Trialogue, Barbara Case

T. V. Love, Jane Comfort Dance Company

Light of the Body, Deborah Hay

AWARDS AND RECOGNITION

Indo-US. Sub commission Travel Grant, 1992

Meet the Composer, 1989

Gold & Multi-Platinum Sales Award Record, 1986, *Graceland*

Gold Sales Award Record, 1983, *Speaking in Tongues*

National Endowment for the Arts Composer Fellowship, 1978-1979

National Endowment for the Arts Video Fellowship, 1975-1976

RESIDENCES

Master Artist, Atlantic Center for the Arts, New Smyrna Beach, FL

Composer in Residence, The Center for the Arts, Stuart, Florida

Master Artist, Memphis Academy of the Arts, Memphis, Tennessee

The Retreat, Ahmedabad, India

Statewide Partnership

Dickie Landry. Composer. Saxophonist. Photographer. Artist. was curated by Susan Moldenhauer, Director & Chief Curator of the University of Wyoming Art Museum. The project included a partnership with three organizations in Jackson Hole, Wyoming, which presented a second exhibition, *Dickie Landry: Explorations in Axonometric Projections*, also curated by Moldenhauer, in addition to a visiting residency by Landry. This was the first time the Arts Association, Dancer's Workshop, Jackson Hole Center for the Arts and the University of Wyoming Art Museum partnered on a major exhibition and artist residency.

ARTS ASSOCIATION

The Art Association has made visual art a vital part of creative life in Jackson Hole for over 52 years. Visual art experiences are provided to more than 2,000 people of all backgrounds in over 300 classes each year. Through classes and exhibits of local, national and international artists, the Art Association brings a vitality to our community.

DANCER'S WORKSHOP

Dancers' Workshop is a thriving non-profit organization in Jackson Hole, Wyoming that presents a rich repertoire of educational experiences and world-class performance opportunities. The School is the essence of Dancers' Workshop, comprised of a top-tier youth program, a pre-professional dance company and a competitive adult dance and fitness program. Our Artists In Residence programs enhance our commitment to art and artistry, inviting dance companies of the highest caliber to infuse our space and expose our students, teachers, community our own resident professional modern dance company to excellence and diversity in dance. Our Statewide Outreach program promotes the arts and education by exploring classroom concepts using movement in a cross-curricular arts integration. Striving to provide diverse pathways of access to people of all ages, interest and ability, Dancers' Workshop values the immense impact that art can have on every individual.

JACKSON HOLE CENTER FOR THE ARTS

The Jackson Hole Center for the Arts is a hub for the artistic, cultural and creative activity in Jackson Hole, Wyoming. We are fueled by innovation, inspired by collaboration and proud to share our 78,000 sq. foot campus with 19 inspired local, regional and state-wide non-profit organizations who call The Center home.

UNIVERSITY OF WYOMING ART MUSEUM

The University of Wyoming Art Museum is the only academic art museum in Wyoming. In addition to collecting and preserving its diverse collection of original art, the Art Museum has a dynamic exhibition program that presents art of the highest quality from around the globe and throughout time that forms the foundation of its interdisciplinary academic, preschool through grade 12 and public programs. Placing art at the center of learning, the University of Wyoming Art Museum encourages interdisciplinary discourse, research, and inquiry-based learning through programs that serve the state through programs and partnerships developed in response to academic and statewide needs.

Acknowledgements

Dickie Landry. Composer. Saxophonist. Photographer. Artist. was a multi-faceted project that included two exhibitions in the opposite corners of Wyoming—Laramie and Jackson Hole—and two visiting residencies, each with a new interpretation of Landry's 1980s theatrical score, *Trialogue.* I would like to thank our partners in Jackson for their interest in making the exhibition and related events possible: Dancers' Workshop, Center for the Arts, and the Art Association of Jackson Hole.

The opportunity for Dickie Landry to re-imagine his original score for *Trialogue* with Babs Case, the original choreographer for the work, was particularly special. For the Laramie performance, Landry and Case worked with art and dance students: Trevor Cook, Maliina Jensen, Jessie Mays, Reanne Rasmusson, Zack Arjour and Molly Markow. Rehearsal assistants included Fran Romo, Jannifer Deckert and Aaron Wood. Lighting Design was provided by Samantha Ryan. Collaborating UW departments on this production include Theater and Dance, Art and Art History, Art Museum, Music and the A&S Auditorium. I would like to recognize and thank the UW faculty who enthusiastically engaged their students in the *Trialogue* programs: Margaret Wilson, dance; Doug Russell and Diana Baumbach, art; and Ann Guzzo, music. I also want to acknowledge the Art Museum staff, each of whom had major roles to play and work to accomplish in making this project a success.

A big thank you to Babs Case, who enthusiastically supported this project and worked tirelessly to ensure new partnerships for the Art Museum in Jackson, and who provide important artistic support for the *Trialogue* performances. On a personal note, what a pleasure to see Case and Landry working together again after so many years.

Thank you to James Surls for introducing Dickie Landry to me and planting the seed for this important project.

Most of all, my sincere thanks to Dickie Landry for your generosity, enthusiasm, and interest in working with me and the University of Wyoming Art Museum to present the first comprehensive exhibition of your work in the visual arts.

Dickie Landry. Composer Saxophonist. Photographer. Artist. was funded in part by an anonymous donor, Edelweiss Funds, Rocky Mountain Power Foundation, University of Wyoming Art Museum Gala Funds, Wyoming Arts Council through the National Endowment for the Arts and the Wyoming State Legislature. *Dickie Landry: An Exploration in Axonometric Projection* funded by Pam Case & Larry Berlin, Center of Wonder, Dancers' Workshop Board of Directors, E/Ye Design, Pamela & Scott Gibson, Polly & Richard Spencer, Tayloe Piggott Gallery, US Bancorp, Barbara & John Vogelstein Foundation, Willow Street Group in memory of Spephen Adamson, Wyoming Art Council and Wyoming Humanities Council.

The University of Wyoming Art Museum is funded in part by Union Wireless; TRONOX; BlueCross BlueShield of Wyoming; BP America; Cloud Peak Energy Resources; First Interstate Bank; Groathouse Construction, Inc.; Ivinson Memorial Hospital; Verizon Wireless; Premier Bone & Joint; Cheyenne Regional Medical Center; Rocky Mountain Power Foundation; the Guthrie Family Foundation; Exxon Mobile Foundation; Mendicino Family Trust; Mary Storer Foundation; UW Foundation; Albany County School District #1; Richard and Judith Agee; Daniel R Anthony; Stephen and Kathleen Beiber; Chris and Kathryn Boswell; Tom and Jacque Buchanan; Ross and Marial Bulmer; Rod and Maxine Chisolm; John and Esther Clay; Roy and Caryl Cline; Barbara Dilts; Patricia R. Guthrie; Mel Cox; E. Jayne Dooley; Jerald and Annie Dukes; Cynthia Kendrick; David Jones and Mary Hardin-Jones; Anthony Mandujano; Richard McGinity and Susan Berman; Frank and Barbara Mendicino; Gary Negich; Nick Murdock; Charles and Reta Ralph; Tom and Sandra Rardin; Pam Rentschler; Phyllis Shelton; Fred Von Ahrens; anonymous sponsors; Wyoming Public Radio; the National Advisory Board of the UW Art Museum; Diane E Bonner Memorial Endowment for Collections, National Advisory Board Endowment, Sherman W & Dorothy Burns Estate Fund, Casper Art Museum Fund, Lisa Lewis Dubois Student Exhibition Award, James T Forrest UW Art Museum Trust, Patricia Guthrie Special Exhibitions Gallery Endowment, Erma M Hill UW Art Museum Endowment, Anonymous Excellence Fund, Robert and Judith Redd Knight Endowment for Conservation and Acquisitions. Frank and Barbara Mendicino Endowment for Collections and Conservation, Ron and Patti Salvagio Endowment for Art Museum Programs. Sigrid See Excellence Fund for the Art Museum Teaching Institute, Ann Simpson and Family Student Exhibition Award; Lucile Wright Endowment; UW Office of the President, UW Office of Government & Community Relations; UW Office of Academic Affairs, UW Division of Administration, UW Office of Student Affairs; UW College of Agriculture and Natural Resources; UW College of Engineering and Applied Science; UW Department of Art; UW Libraries; UW Outreach School; UW MFA Creative Writing; Wyoming Community Foundation; and the Wyoming State Legislature; by grants from the National Endowment for the Humanities and the Wyoming Arts Council through the Wyoming State Legislature and the National Endowment for the Arts; and through the generosity of many individuals and businesses.